Becoming a Historian

A Survival Manual

2003 Edition by

Melanie S. Gustafson

Published by the Committee on Women Historians and the American Historical Association

2000 Committee on Women Historians

Elizabeth Lunbeck, *chair*, Princeton University; Guido Ruggeiro, Penn State University; Sandra Treadway, Library of Virginia; Ann Waltner, University of Minnesota; Susan Pearson, graduate student representative, University of North Carolina; Virginia Sanchez-Korrol, Brooklyn College, CUNY; Noralee Frankel, assistant director of women and minorities, American Historical Association; Arnita Jones, executive director, American Historical Association, *ex officio*.

MELANIE GUSTAFSON is an associate professor of history at the University of Vermont, where she teaches U.S. history and women's history. Her current scholarship focuses on the history of women and American political parties.

AHA Editors: Kate Masur
                  Robert Townsend

Editorial Assistants: Miriam Hauss
                           Liz Townsend

Layout: Flannery A. Shaughnessy
             Chris Hale

CONTENTS

❖ PREFACE ❖

IN 1975, RECOGNIZING THAT UNWRITTEN RULES IN THE HISTORICAL PROFESSION often lead to inequality, the American Historical Association's Committee on Women Historians put together the first edition of this manual. Its focus was evident in its title, a *Manual for Women (And Other) Historians.* The name changes in 1991 to *Becoming a Historian: A Manual for Women and Men* and in 2002 to *Becoming a Historian: A Survival Manual* reflecting its change in scope. This is a manual for all historians at various stages of their careers. Its aim is to provide practical information that will help historians as they enter new phases of their careers.

Over the years, many individuals have contributed to the writing of this manual. The first version was prepared by the 1975 Committee on Women Historians (CWH): Mary Frances Berry, Carl Degler, Mary Jane Hamilton, Joan Kelly, Linda K. Kerber, Suzanne Lebsock, Jane DeHart Mathews, Emiliana P. Noether, and Marie Perinbam. Otis Graham and Dorothy Ross provided assistance. The second edition was prepared by the 1979 CWH: Judith Babbitts, Mary O. Furner, Rosalyn Terborg-Penn, Martha Toplin, Joan W. Scott, and Sydney V. James, who rewrote many sections of the text. They were assisted by Linda K. Kerber, Evan A. Thomas, Barry Karl, Janet W. James, Noralee Frankel, and Phyllis D. Keller. Incorporating material from the previous versions into a new edition was the job of the 1989 CWH: Barbara Engel, Joan Jensen, Louise Kerr, Barbara Melosh, Robert Moeller, and Melanie Gustafson, who again rewrote much of the text. Contributing significant sections to that version, now included in this new edition, were Linda Arnold, Paul Boyer, Barbara Engel, Linda Gordon, Cynthia Harrison, Barbara Howe, Joan Jensen, Barbara Melosh, and Robert Moeller. Noralee Frankel, Roxanne Myers Spencer, and Ellen Broidy provided editorial assistance.

This edition, initiated by the 2000 CWH, has benefited from the contribution of Steven A. Leibo, whose December 1995 article in *Perspectives*, "Using the Annual Meeting to Win a Position at a Small Undergraduate College," is partly reprinted in Chapter 7. Also contributing to the cooperative nature of this enterprise is the exchange between the AHA and the Canadian Historical Association (CHA). Canadian readers of this manual may be aware of their

Becoming a Historian. That manual is an augmented version of the 1989 AHA edition, while this new AHA edition has benefited from the insights and additions made by the Canadian editors, Franca Iacovetta and Molly Ladd Taylor. Editorial assistance for this edition was also provided by Edmund Abaka, Lykke de la Cour, Lisa Dillon, Stephen Heathorn, Lorraine O'Donnell, Adele Perry, Richard Bond, Chris Hale, Kate Masur, and Frances Clarke.

In reissuing this manual, we hope to introduce you to the profession as a whole and to help you navigate the various phases of your career, from the first decision to apply to graduate school through the tenure and promotion process. While not every section of the manual may be relevant to your immediate needs, we encourage all historians to read the entire manual at least once to get a sense of the needs of colleagues who are at different points in their careers. We believe the manual will help you with concerns specific to your situation and will also help you to be a better colleague.

❖ 1 ❖

WHAT MAKES HISTORY A PROFESSION?

A PROFESSION IMPLIES AN ORGANIZATION, USUALLY QUITE AN ELABORATE ONE. Collectively, the practitioners decide upon their responsibilities and work to maintain appropriate standards. In universities, groups of professional people accept candidates, train them, and decide when they are ready to practice. Successful candidates join associations, ordinarily of regional or national dimensions, but often with international ties, such as the Organization of American Historians, the National Council on Public History, or the American Historical Association. Collectively, the practitioners evaluate one another's contributions to learning. Professional solidarity calls for evaluating other historians purely on the basis of their performance as historians. All historians are obliged to keep abreast of the publication of new discoveries, carry forward research, evaluate other historians' work, participate in professional organizations, and disseminate historical knowledge.

CODE OF ETHICS

Like other professions, the historical profession has its own ethics. For historians, whose work is interpreting the human past, the first canon of ethics requires accuracy in its fullest sense. It is the duty of the professional to understand how the canons of accuracy, honesty, thoroughness, freedom from bias, and other ethical considerations are evaluated and defined within the profession. Publications defining these ethics include the American Historical Association's *Statement on Standards of Professional Conduct* and the National Council on Public History's "Ethical Guidelines for the Historian." (See Appendix B for web addresses and contact information.)

REPRESENTING THE PROFESSION

Historians have an obligation to promote the profession both internally (to students and colleagues) and externally (to the public at large). Such professional service entails a host of corollary duties. Some are profession-wide, such as advancing knowledge and putting it before the public. Other duties are more specific to the particular positions in the profession. Teachers must teach, editors must edit, and managers must manage in ways that satisfy the legitimate expectations of those who count on benefits from these services. This moral obligation to serve creates a special relationship between work and pay, and between the profession and the public. Our duties continue, regardless of the hours, until we have done our best to achieve professionally satisfactory results.

A working historian becomes part not only of the profession but also of the larger academy. While disciplinary boundaries seem to be rigid at the university level, many individuals find that they often cross these boundaries as they conduct research, engage in debates, and build their communities and support networks. Interdisciplinary connection is particularly common for historians who concentrate in women's history, ethnic history, gay and lesbian history, and area studies. As a result, multidisciplinary groups defined by thematic interests have developed within the academy. Many historians will find that these multi- or interdisciplinary groups provide them with an additional professional community that suits their academic and professional interests. In addition, public historians often find opportunities for scholarly engagement in interdisciplinary seminars held within public agencies or set up independently by scholars in a community.

External promotion is advanced by encouraging the study of history and by seeking public support for higher education, research, and historic preservation. Write to your congressional representative or senator to support larger appropriations for colleges and universities and for cultural endowments. Such efforts may also be effective in getting more historians employed.

The long hours many historians put into their careers result not only from their obligation to the profession and their interest in the past, but also from their understanding that they are part of a larger community working to make the world a more humane place. Historians are not so narrowly focused that all they do is eat, sleep, and think history. All historians have other interests and responsibilities. Still, the career of the professional historian sounds demanding. It is. It sounds as though it requires uncommon self-discipline. It does. It also, however, offers priceless rewards: a degree of professional autonomy and the satisfaction in performing services that few other professions can offer. This manual provides historians with outlines and gauges for success in the diverse roles that they will play as professionals throughout their careers.

❖ 2 ❖

How to Apply to Graduate School

Deciding to Apply

To be accepted as a graduate student in history, start planning your applications almost a year before you wish to enroll. Ordinarily that means in the autumn of your senior year in college. Deadlines for applications vary from early December to February, sometimes later. Plan to take tests, such as the Graduate Record Examination (GRE), as early as possible because most schools want to see test scores with your application. Try to take the GRE in October but definitely take it by December. You need not give up hope if you take tests later, but you should realize that the main part of the selection process would be over by the time your scores become available. Most graduate fellowships are awarded in March, in time for the general announcement of admission in April.

Gathering Information and Applications

Ask your undergraduate professors for information and find out if they will put in a good word for you with acquaintances in graduate departments. To get the most useful responses about graduate programs from your professors, pose questions in ways that allow for straightforward answers. Ask your professors which schools they think offer the best programs for your interests and abilities. Do not hesitate to seek out professors' advice, even if you have not taken classes with them. If you know someone who studied at a school you are interested in, that advice may be particularly valuable. Your undergraduate catalog will often list where faculty members did their graduate work.

The American Historical Association's *Directory of History Departments, Historical Organizations, and Historians* is usually available in your undergraduate school's history department office, or this information can be obtained from the AHA web site at http://www.theaha.org. The *Directory* provides information on almost all graduate history departments in the United States. Inclusion in the *Directory* is by subscription, so a few institutions are not represented, but by and large this is a very comprehensive resource. You can find other educational directories, such as Barron's *Profiles of American Colleges* and Peterson's *Guide to Graduate and Professional Schools*, at your college or public library. Look at graduate school catalogs as well. Catalogs list courses offered, as well as admissions, degree, tuition, and financial aid requirements. Most of the information will be up-to-date, although changes in tuition rates and course offerings are frequent. You should be able to find catalogs in your school or public library or on the web. If not, the schools you are interested in will send them, although some graduate programs will send a catalog only after receiving an application or a fee. Try to collect catalogs from schools the summer before you begin the application process so that you can think about your choice. Most departments now have a web site that provides current information on course offerings, admission requirements, and tuition and financial aid. In addition, the site may provide links to professors' own web pages or mailboxes.

As you talk to professors you know, some will speak frankly about the strengths and weaknesses of particular departments or faculty members. Others may drop hints. Listen carefully for hints about department politics or personality clashes. You don't want to wind up in a department where the two people you want to work with haven't spoken to each other in a decade.

To apply, you must have the necessary forms. These are available by contacting the individual schools. Address your request to the director of graduate admissions or the department of history if you cannot find a specific name. You will receive in reply a packet of forms and information. Then your real work begins.

WHAT TO LOOK FOR IN A PROGRAM, DEPARTMENT, AND SCHOOL

Remember that you will be spending at least two years, and probably far longer, in the graduate program and department. The average number of years to complete the PhD in history is eight. Therefore, you should learn as much as you can about specific aspects of the department, its programs, and the institution. The following points will help you with decision-making at both the application and selection stages.

The location of the university may be a factor in where you choose to apply. Some students cannot or prefer not to relocate; others are limited to schools in certain regions or where there are job opportunities for their partners; still others don't care where they live, as long as the library is close by. If you cannot relocate, you may find yourself with several degrees from the same institution. Opinions vary on whether this might pose a problem in your career. It is definitely to your advantage to work with several professors in more than one university. If you know you want to continue at your undergraduate institution for your PhD, for example, you should consider going somewhere else for the MA. On the other hand, don't worry if this is impossible. To a large extent, graduate study—and your career in history—is what you make it.

Explore special programs such as those in archival management or women's history. For those interested in a history career outside of the academy, there are also many programs in public history. If you are attracted by a special program within a department, such as legal history or the history of technology, do your best to find out whether the program is securely established. If you expect to depend heavily on one or two faculty members, find out about their status. Professors often leave for sabbaticals, move to other campuses or colleges, or retire. If your decision is based on a particular faculty member, know whether there is a backup person to work with should that professor leave. This becomes particularly important as you begin to select among the schools that have accepted you.

Find out about the dissertation topics and placement of recent graduates by looking at placement records, if they are available, or by asking the graduate advisor. Look at a list of recent dissertations, which the department should have available. For an overall view of recent PhDs, see the AHA's annual *Directory of History Departments, Historical Organizations, and Historians,* and *Dissertation Abstracts,* published monthly by University Microfilms International, Inc. (UMI). *Dissertation Abstracts* includes abstracts of doctoral dissertations submitted to UMI by 550 participating institutions, and it is available in most university libraries. Consult back issues of the Organization of American Historians' *Journal of American History,* which lists dissertations in American history. Dissertations granted within a department will reflect both faculty interests and the facilities available.

Research financial aid and awards. Read the catalogs and any departmental brochures you can find. It is likely that only some awards are channeled through the department. Do you need different forms to apply to different grant offices? Find out if a first-year financial aid commitment is for one time only or if it means that the department is committed to funding every year of your course work. Is there funding for dissertation research? You should weigh the nature of the financial aid package with the quality of the school. If possible, don't just go to the institution that offers you the most money.

If you plan to supplement your stipend (should it be awarded) with student loans, you will have to file financial aid forms with the financial aid office at each school. Most often these forms should be filed as soon as possible after the first of January. The sooner you file these forms the better. Most schools require additional information, such as a copy of your most recent tax return and other verification materials. Each school's policy is different and you should contact the proper personnel for further information and forms. Do not rely solely on what the history department tells you; call the financial aid office directly. The forms used by schools include the Family Financial Statement from the American College Testing Program, and the Financial Aid Form, or Graduate and

Professional School Financial Aid Service forms, which are available from the schools' financial aid offices. Know which forms the schools you are applying to require. You might want to send your financial aid applications by registered mail, so you have proof of receipt in case of a financial dispute. Do not wait to be accepted to file these forms or you might miss important deadlines.

Although most financial aid packages require you to enroll as a full-time student, some people go to graduate school part time for economic or personal reasons. Being a part-time student does not mean that you are less committed to graduate study, and part-timers have the right to the same education as full-time students. Besides, "full time" does not mean "all the time." Many full-time students have family responsibilities, and most have to work for wages at some point during their graduate education. Nevertheless, graduate study requires a big commitment.

It is not easy to do graduate course work and exam preparation on a part-time basis, and it is even more difficult (though not impossible) to successfully complete a dissertation part time. You will not be able to earn a PhD "on the side" if you already have a demanding career. Moreover, you may miss the intellectual community of graduate school if you are not at the university during the day. Part-time students may have to make a special effort to break down isolation and meet other grad students.

Clarify differences in the requirements for MA, PhD, and other special programs. Which should you be applying for? Is the master's degree a terminal degree or the first step toward the PhD? Is there flexibility in the program requirements? What are the language requirements? If there are language requirements, try to meet them before you begin the graduate program.

Once you have become familiar with a school's official publications, don't hesitate to write, call, or visit to get further information. If you plan to visit a school, go to the best school for your purposes, not simply one that is cheaper or closer to where you are living when you apply. This is not the time to base your decisions on short-term goals. If you cannot visit, contact the faculty member whose field is nearest to your interests. You can find out individual faculty members' office hours from the department. You might also ask the graduate secretary for names of current students in those programs. Students may give you a more candid assessment of the program's strengths and weaknesses. From these individuals, you can ask about resources for graduate students. Does the library have extensive holdings? Are there computers available for students? These resources indicate the level of commitment within the department and school. Make as informed a decision as possible.

Attempt to build relationships with prospective faculty advisors. Write to faculty members with whom you would most likely work. This initial letter should explain the kind of research you would like to do and perhaps include a copy of your statement of purpose. Even if these faculty advisors are not on the admissions committee, they might be able to go to bat for promising applicants.

After you have visited a department, met with professors, talked with graduate students, and gotten a feel for the community, write to thank people you met. Remember, no matter what school you attend, these individuals will be your professional colleagues, so start building goodwill now.

THE APPLICATION PROCESS

Application instructions will vary with each institution, so read each set with care. Once your application arrives at the university, it becomes a file (composed of your statement of purpose, writing sample, letters of recommendation, and transcript). That file may be read by all members of the department, by every professor in your field, or by a small committee of faculty members (and sometimes graduate students) with several different specialties. All members of the department you send it to may scrutinize your application, but usually a committee will examine it. Graduate admissions committees look for students who have a lively interest in history. Unlike college recruiters, they are seldom scouting for leadership talents or well-rounded persons. To increase your chances of acceptance, make scholarship the focal point of your application.

TIPS ON THE PERSONAL STATEMENT AND LETTERS OF RECOMMENDATION

Together with the academic transcript and (in some cases) GRE scores, the most important components of an application for graduate study in history are, for many history departments, the student's own statement of purpose, the supporting letters of recommendation, and a writing sample. Here are some suggestions for avoiding common pitfalls and for making your materials as strong and persuasive as possible.

The most effective statement of purpose is specific, well written, professional in tone, scrupulously accurate in spelling and grammar, and tailored to each institution. The statement should avoid sweeping philosophical generalizations, avowals of political or other ideology, or ruminations about the nature of historical knowledge and its essential role in bettering the human condition. No matter how earnestly intended or passionately felt, such lofty rhetoric all too easily descends to the level of cliché, especially when offered in a necessarily compressed form, suggesting an immature and jejune outlook rather than the intended profundity. The statement should also avoid mention of extracurricular activities and achievements, no matter how outstanding, unless they have a direct bearing on the professional field to which you are seeking entry.

While it is certainly appropriate to discuss how you became interested in history, and to include something about your long-range career goals, such matters should be kept brief and to the point. Remember that your application is one of many being read by busy faculty members with many other time-consuming obligations. Keep your tendencies toward loquaciousness well in check, and strictly observe word limits.

A strong statement sums up your scholarly interests and immediate academic objectives in a clear and straightforward fashion. It should be quite precise about the time period, geographic region, or kind of history you want to study, and perhaps even the specific topic you wish ultimately to investigate. You should briefly indicate how your undergraduate reading, research, and course work have shaped your particular interests and prepared you to pursue them further. At the same time, bear in mind that the earlier phases of graduate education involve primarily general training rather than research on a specific topic. Therefore, your statement should convey an openness to the acquisition of a wide range of historical knowledge and research skills rather than an obsessive fixation on a single narrow topic. (An application from a college senior whose sole purpose in life is to study the Battle of Antietam or the fall of Malacca to the Portuguese in 1511 would probably raise warning signals for most graduate admissions committees because the student may appear too rigid and narrow.)

It is entirely appropriate, indeed desirable, to tailor your statement of purpose to the institution to which you are applying. Feel free, for example, to mention professors with whom you would like to work, or specific strengths—such as particular manuscript holdings or degree programs—that make the institution attractive to you. Such specificity should avoid elaborate praise or flattery, however; a fawning, excessively deferential tone is likely to be counterproductive.

The statement of purpose is also the place for you to address briefly any anomalies or ambiguities in your record that might give an admissions committee pause, such as a nonstandard grading system or courses whose content is not clear from the transcript (such as "Independent Study"). If your undergraduate background in history is weak, it might be advisable for you to describe in more detail the evolution of your academic interests and to make plain that your commitment to the discipline is now firm.

The quality of the essay is probably more important than its substantive content. The members of the admissions committee who read your application will evaluate your statement for the evidence it offers about the quality, clarity, and originality of your mind; your maturity and sense of direction; your skills as a writer; and your capacity for careful attention to detail. A thoughtful, well-crafted, coherently organized essay can go a long way toward favorably disposing a committee on your behalf. Conversely, a shallow, formulaic, hastily written statement marred by poor organization, awkwardness of expression, or (even worse) outright grammatical errors or misspellings can seriously undermine an otherwise strong application. There have been instances of application essays where misspelled words or grammatical errors were heavily circled or underlined by readers, with an exclamation point in the margin. Such lapses of detail are not necessarily fatal in themselves, particularly if the admissions committee convinces itself that the applicant is "a diamond in the rough." But such errors are sufficiently damaging, especially in borderline cases, that every effort to avoid such mistakes is strongly recommended.

Letters of recommendation are also highly important. You should select with great care the professors you ask to write on your behalf. While you obviously cannot quiz someone in detail about the content of a letter of recommendation, it is acceptable for you to ask in advance whether the professor feels able to write a reasonably positive letter. If possible, select faculty members whose scholarly work might be known to those who will be reading the letters. (Admissions committees evaluate the writers of recommendation letters as well as the subject of those letters!) Sometimes, particularly at large institutions, it is junior faculty members, or even graduate teaching assistants, who know the applicant best and who write the most useful and perceptive letters. Where feasible, however, try to supplement letters from beginning or relatively unknown instructors with others from more established scholars.

Generally speaking, try to secure a letter of recommendation as soon as possible after you have completed a course or independent study project, when you and your work are still fresh in the instructor's mind. If you wish to obtain a letter from a professor with whom you studied a year or so in the past, or who taught you in a large lecture course, spend a little time talking about your work in the course, your general undergraduate program, and your scholarly interests to refresh the instructor's memory and fix yourself more precisely in the writer's mind. The more specific a letter of recommendation, the greater the weight it carries. Even if you know a professor well, it will not hurt to provide your statement of purpose, curriculum vitae (including grade point average and any scholastic honors achieved), and a personal assessment of your goals and ability to fulfill them. It is also a good idea to give the professor a copy of exams or a paper you wrote in the course.

Do not hesitate to ask for a letter of recommendation; writing these letters is part of a professor's job. At the same time, do be considerate and talk to the professor in person. Make sure your forms are filled out properly, and always include a stamped, addressed envelope. Most important, allow ample time, preferably four weeks, before the deadlines. As the deadline approaches, verify that the school received your letters. You may need to give your referee a gentle reminder of the deadlines.

A writing sample forms another crucial part of the application for almost all universities. Ideally, you should submit a paper in your chosen field that demonstrates your ability to do research using primary sources.

Clearly, no single formula can guarantee admission to a graduate school in history or any other discipline. Each decision reflects a variety of factors and subjective judgments by fallible human beings.

Admissions committees must match student interests with faculty expertise and try to balance the number of students in any given field. No matter how talented you are, you are unlikely to be accepted into a program that cannot accommodate your interests, either because the specialist in your area is on leave or because the field is simply not covered. That is one reason it is so important to research what institution is best for you.

KEEPING TRACK OF APPLICATIONS AND DEADLINES

Keep track of application forms, deadlines, and other correspondence. The worst thing about applying to graduate school is the bureaucracy. There are so many different forms that it is important to keep some kind of organized file or you will be easily overwhelmed. Keep all application materials in a file folder. On the inside cover, keep track of each school's requirements and your follow-up. Photocopy all materials you send out, including letters to faculty and graduate students.

TRANSCRIPTS

You will be asked to send transcripts or to have your college send them as soon as possible. If your transcript does not follow a standard format, ensure that it is accompanied by a description. If courses are listed in obscure abbreviations, send along a prose description of what you have studied.

TEST SCORES

If you are unhappy with your initial GRE score, take the test again. Experience commonly results in a higher score. To find out about the GRE, contact the Educational Testing Service (see Appendix B, page 86). Information about the GRE can also be found at most campus career centers.

SET YOUR SIGHTS HIGH

After determining which graduate programs you are interested in, apply to your first choice and several alternatives. Consider applying to universities of varying prestige, including "safety" schools as well as those more difficult to get into. Don't sell yourself short by assuming that the better-known departments won't accept you or give you aid. They often take more students and have more scholarship money than smaller, lesser-known institutions. If you are not accepted the first time you apply, you can always try again next year. You will be competing in a different pool of applicants and may have a better chance. Good luck!

❖ 3 ❖

GRADUATE STUDY

IN MOST MA AND PHD PROGRAMS, YOU ARE EXPECTED TO LEARN AN enormous amount about several loosely defined fields of history, pass a series of demanding exams, and then write an original thesis or dissertation. There are variations on this pattern, which may be a reason to choose a certain university.

It is important to understand what will be required of you in graduate school. Yet clear advice is sometimes scarce. At times, it may seem like graduate school operates according to a secret code of behavior that is never explained but by which you are constantly judged. While graduate schools vary significantly from program to program, all ask that students approach their work with a seriousness and commitment not required by undergraduate programs. There is usually less emphasis on learning "the facts" (though it is assumed that you will eventually master them) and more emphasis on interpretation, analysis, and historiography than in most undergraduate history courses. Graduate students are also introduced to research techniques, the art of scholarly criticism, and other intricacies of historical and scholarly practice.

You should understand the structure and goals of the program you have entered. There are basic differences between master's and PhD programs. Most master's programs usually involve a year or two of course work and a final master's thesis. Some programs do not require a thesis but may require additional credit hours and a written or oral examination. PhD programs generally involve course work, written and/or oral comprehensive examinations, language requirements, and a dissertation and its defense. In addition to the academic program, graduate students also work as teaching assistants, research assistants, or part-time instructors. The discussion below deals largely with PhD programs, but the comments can apply, in modified form, to MA programs. Requirements vary, so it is important to know what is expected of you at different phases of your graduate career.

11

Consult your department's guidelines, your advisor, the director of graduate studies, and other students on how to pick the fields in which you will concentrate. Fields of study are usually divided according to topic, region, and time period. Departments may relax some requirements if you present viable reasons, so think freely about what will be beneficial. One way to approach your field of study is to think of the subject you want to specialize in and then choose areas that fit well around it. As you begin, you might define your field as European. As you study more, you may become a modern European scholar and concentrate on labor and gender. Try to make plans early to avoid scattering your efforts, but remain receptive to new possibilities. You might develop enthusiasm for a topic that used to bore you. Overall, you should know the requirements for the fields you have chosen, including languages or field study.

Course Work

Reading or Research Seminars

These are virtually universal in graduate study. Research courses allow you to learn by doing. The grade is based almost entirely on a long paper, which should be the result of original research. Reading courses often require a paper analyzing what you have read, as well as discussion on those readings. Seminars are valuable opportunities to learn about methodology, bibliography, historiography, and philosophy in different fields of history. The program probably requires you to take a small number of seminars, and you should view them as an opportunity to expand and refine your historical skills. Not only are they uniquely valuable in graduate education, but they can get you started toward publication. Intimidating though this idea may be, aim at writing a publishable article in each research seminar. For more advice on publishing, see Chapter 13. You may succeed.

Graduate seminars are also where faculty and students first get to know each other as colleagues and are the main way that graduate students are introduced to scholarly culture. You will be exposed to a wide variety of views, both in your reading and from students and faculty. You will learn to think analytically and to criticize, rather than merely dismiss or trash the scholarship of other historians. You will also receive criticism of your own research and analysis. Vicious or vindictive criticism is unproductive, but you should be tough-skinned about feedback. Use it to improve your work. Often, courses are the main vehicle for building community among graduate students, and classmates may form the core of your social and intellectual groups for years to come.

Course work can also be a difficult and confusing experience. Students often compete with each other for faculty attention. Professors sometimes favor certain students or particular viewpoints and belittle other students and perspectives. In courses where grades are awarded, students often struggle for good evaluations, sometimes sacrificing intellectual development or positive group dynamics.

Students with particular viewpoints, identities, or interests can be especially marginalized in weekly seminars. Some women students find certain male students obstreperous and seminar environments aggressive and intimidating. Students from different class, ethnic, racial, or linguistic backgrounds can face difficulties in articulating their concerns in courses, as can gay and lesbian students. Most graduate students are often unsure about what, exactly, they are supposed to demonstrate in courses: are they there to learn or to show how much they already know?

When combined with demanding workloads, these pedagogical and interpersonal difficulties can be trying indeed. Furthermore, the most intense phase of course work occurs in the first years of graduate school, when many students are settling into a new city or country, coping with separation from family and friends, perhaps negotiating a long-distance relationship, and generally adjusting to a new environment with new pressures and demands. As a result, students often feel isolated and confused.

Try to use the opportunities presented by course work without getting bogged down by its problems and difficulties. Remember that your courses are not the sum total of your intellectual life, and learn what you can from the professor and the reading list and assignments. You do not need to "know" everything and should not lose sleep trying to anticipate what the professor will ask or want to hear. Most faculty want some indication that you have engaged the literature and have some interesting or intelligent things to say about it. Treat the other students with respect, and try to both give and receive helpful criticism without being harsh or overly sensitive. Courses should be places for collective learning and informed debate, not battlefields.

While most of your course work will be in the history department, classes offered by other departments or interdisciplinary programs will often be extremely useful in building your critical and research skills as well as in offering you intellectual stimulation and the opportunity to meet new colleagues. If given the opportunity to take methodological or theoretical courses, such as web design or cultural studies, do so. Even if your own work does not rely on these techniques, you will find them useful for understanding the work of other scholars.

COMPREHENSIVE EXAMINATIONS

As you complete your course work, you will be ready to start thinking about taking your comprehensive or qualifying exams. Examinations offer you the opportunity to sift through long periods of history and to construct your own interpretations. Whatever the form of the exam—oral, written, or both—it will seem terrifying. Other graduate students will regale you with ghastly tales of what they went through. Gathering this fund of anecdotes and scanning your patchwork of preparation, you might conclude that you ought to put off the terrible day. However, watch other successful graduate students. How long do they study? How much information seems required to pass? As you study for your exams, ask your prospective examiners what they expect. Professors know it is easy to find out what a student does not know. Most want to find a topic a candidate can talk about intelligently, so they will probably offer you some clues in advance. Examiners will be as interested in your ability to articulate your own opinions as they are in your ability to recount others' interpretations accurately.

Most faculty see the comps largely as an exercise in self-directed reading, but individual professors differ in how they see their role in the process. Some meet with students on a weekly or monthly basis; others agree to a few meetings. Many departments now keep former exams on file, so check out this possibility. Consult with senior students about their exams. You can form a study group and do mock exams and other trial exercises. Most important, keep in regular contact with your examiners throughout the preparation. Let them know about your progress and any problems you encounter. Try to enjoy your reading, try to concentrate on what you do know, and avoid panicking about what you have yet to learn. Steel yourself and set a date for your examination.

If you fail an exam, remember that it is not the end of the world. Most departments will let you try again. Find out why your committee was unsatisfied with your performance. At the same time, learn about your rights by consulting the department and school of graduate studies. With these factors in mind, develop a strategy for dealing with the problem; consult sympathetic faculty members and administrators. At worst, comprehensive examinations are something to struggle through. At best, they are useful vehicles for mastering several bodies of historical literature capped by a satisfying moment of public recognition. If your committee wants to take you out for lunch or dinner after you have passed your comps, enjoy the event. For most of us, these are the last set of exams we will ever have to write.

THE DISSERTATION

Your dissertation is where you make an individual mark as a scholar. It is your dissertation, moreover, that will most clearly define your career and how others in the historical profession see you. The completion of an interesting, well-executed dissertation in a timely manner will most directly determine your success on the academic job market. Do not expect the dissertation to be like just another research paper or book. The subject of the dissertation is not just your topic, it is also you—your dedication, your acumen, your research skills, and your familiarity with the secondary literature. In the dissertation you will need to present new and original research in primary sources, demonstrating a clear and detailed understanding of the secondary literature, while also striking out in new directions.

CHOOSING A TOPIC

Once you have passed the big exams, or even before that, you must select a dissertation topic. You should work on a topic that fits into current scholarly trends but also explores new perspectives and finds a unique niche. Your dissertation topic indicates to colleagues your research and teaching interests. This choice will determine what will occupy your thoughts for the next several years and may govern where you live for a while. Obviously, the subject will determine the limits of what you can say about it and the concepts you can use. You will also need accessible primary sources that yield sufficient information. Scout out possibilities early. Work closely with your advisor in both choosing and developing your topic. Your advisor will help you shape an idea into a workable project. Ideally, a student's reputation is made by the dissertation. A special distinction may be accorded for thinking up an original subject. Make your own choice, rather than accepting a topic chosen by your advisor, and widen the possibilities to include a first-rate discovery rather than a humdrum rehashing or an improbable interpretation.

All history students can benefit from working with faculty advisors outside the history department. In fact, many departments now require an outside dissertation reader who is not a historian. Knowing faculty in other departments will expand any history student's outlook and can help when it's time to form a dissertation committee.

For students of color, women students, and gay or lesbian students in particular, connecting with faculty outside the history department can be crucial. Such students may face special challenges in finding good mentoring. Some advisors still offer such students poor guidance because they are convinced, perhaps subconsciously, that these students lack creativity and will not do justice to significant topics.

Many women graduate students have been strongly encouraged by advisors either to choose or to avoid work in women's history. Ignorance as well as misogyny may lie behind such advice. Likewise, faculty may stereotype students of color and gay/lesbian students, assuming too quickly that they are only interested in scholarship relating to what they perceive as the student's group identity.

Students who meet with stereotyping assumptions or who simply cannot find the advice they need in the history department should look beyond their departmental advisors for fresh perspectives (and more respect) during course work and as they develop their dissertation proposal. Faculty in other departments can provide support and encouragement. They may also have helpful suggestions for on-campus mentors or study and support groups. Even if a history advisor is very receptive to a student's ideas, non-history faculty may provide new insights or assist with connections to scholarly networks.

Students in search of mentors might also look to other institutions for help. You may want to look at the most recent edition of the AHA's annual *Directory of History Departments, Historical Organizations, and Historians* or university web sites to find outside mentors. Occasionally, faculty or other professionals outside students' home institutions have become informal mentors and have read drafts of students' work and conferred with them at conferences and other professional meetings. Your school might also permit a non-faculty advisor to sit on your dissertation committee.

THE DISSERTATION PROPOSAL

Many departments want you to submit a plan of action on your subject, often called the dissertation proposal. The idea is to prevent students from trying impossible projects that would never win final approval. Some faculty members might even have doubts about a viable proposal, but these objections are often based on sketchy knowledge and can be overcome with more details. If opposition seems likely, plan to enlist the aid of your supervisor in pursuing tactics that will gain approval of your prospectus. You may be asked to present your plans in writing, orally, or both. Preparing the proposal will help clarify your thoughts. You want your prospectus to offer a clear research outline covering the subject you intend to pursue, how you intend to do so, and what conclusions you expect to reach. While your teachers will evaluate your past work when writing letters of recommendation for grants, your proposal is their only guide to your current course of study.

Realize that there is an element of projection in the exercise. If you knew how the work would turn out, it would not be worth doing. What you forecast is only an educated guess, but it is an important baseline. Establishing clear working hypotheses—even if you ultimately abandon or reject them—offer a way for you to get on with the initial stages of your research. The project almost surely will reshape itself as your work progresses.

Ask to see samples of successful dissertation proposals written for your department. You may find that one of the most common formats used in your department is a narrative of speculative questions that lead to the hypothesis. After looking over one or two proposals, ask the writers, if possible, whether they have turned their proposals into grant applications. There are numerous grants available for doctoral students. Ask your graduate advisor for help in locating sources and see Chapter 5, Funding Graduate and Postdoctoral Study.

BEGINNING THE DISSERTATION

Whatever subject you choose for a dissertation, however you get advice, you must research and write it. You will probably find that your relationships with faculty change dramatically as you move from course work to the dissertation. Speak to your advisor and clarify expectations about how you will proceed.

Maintaining a good working relationship with your advisor is essential and, for good or ill, it is chiefly up to you to accommodate the relationship. Remember that your advisor, at this point, knows more than you do about writing history.

As you form your dissertation committee, consider not only faculty members' intellectual strengths, but also their interpersonal styles. You may want to try balancing different qualities, such as supportiveness, tendencies to intervene or allow independent work, intellectual engagement, and the like. Discuss the makeup of the committee with your advisor.

When you begin your research, you must gather and analyze the data. You may want to talk with colleagues about strategies for gathering and organizing information, including computer programs that have proven especially useful for history research. Procedures vary from one project to another, and yet the temptation almost always arises to keep going, to find out every last detail, to look at every conceivable source, to try all imaginable statistical devices. At some point, you have to stop gathering information and start writing. In virtually all projects the time comes when the yield from your efforts shrinks noticeably. You may not have learned all there is to learn but you have learned enough. In any case, this point of diminishing returns is the place to stop research and start composing a text. Don't feel that you have to begin at the beginning. Start with the section you feel most confident about. The introduction often will be the last thing you write.

How you present your work to your supervisor, of course, is not wholly in your control. You may be called upon to hand in chapters at regular intervals. Beware of spending your time digesting your advisor's comments and revising the parts you've already written. While you need input as you research and write, it may be better to write a first draft of the whole thing, if your advisor will be content with this procedure. Then you can revise it as a whole. And you will revise. But be aware that if your advisor sets different rules, you will have to comply.

MAKING PROGRESS

The dissertation is the last stage of your graduate study. Don't let it become a stumbling block. It is not wise to put off making a living forever, and it becomes demoralizing to drag out your stay at graduate school. There are also professional reasons: Potential employers look at how long you took to complete your degree. They want an employee who gets things done.

Try to overcome the isolation of daily dissertation work. Group support, formal or casual, can be the key to success and survival. Lunches at the archives have sustained many a historian-in-training. Informal student groups dedicated to the helpful discussion of works-in-progress often prove a crucial place for developing ideas and work in a supportive environment, as can more formal research seminars. Some people with "writer's block" find it useful to be given concrete deadlines to meet. Others have made use of any variety of helpful hints;

your university probably has counselors to help with serious writing difficulties. Students researching and writing far from their home institutions are especially prone to isolation and may want to seek out other institutional settings to provide guidance or structure.

While parents of young children, or others with exceptional circumstances, may have good reasons for taking longer than usual to get a degree, it is important to proceed efficiently. If, however, you find yourself unable to focus exclusively on your studies, don't feel as though you don't belong in the profession. Do not assume that delay is a personal failure; rather, try to tap into available resources to both allow you to meet existing requirements and to alter them to realistically suit your situation.

Graduate study in history can be confusing and taxing. But it can also be a highly rewarding experience. Capitalizing on the benefits and minimizing the difficulties of graduate school will help you navigate this stage and focus on the interests that led you to history in the first place.

❖ 4 ❖

ACADEMIC RELATIONSHIPS

STUDENT RELATIONSHIPS

YOU WILL LEARN A GREAT DEAL FROM OTHER GRADUATE STUDENTS. YOU WILL MEET veterans as well as beginners. You will find out what lies ahead of you, and you will learn about the unwritten rules of department life.

Graduate life should be characterized by intellectual give-and-take. Do what you can to make the company of other graduate students pleasant and intellectually rewarding by cultivating friendships with graduate students whose ideas and insights you appreciate. In addition to students in your department, seek out students with similar interests in other departments. These people will listen to your ideas, read your papers, hear rehearsals of your public performances, offer opinions of your efforts, argue with you—and you must do the same for them—all without exposing anyone in the group to undue mental wear and tear. Such friendships often last a lifetime.

Opportunities exist to expand your network of graduate student colleagues throughout the United States. A number of professional organizations facilitate such interaction, including the Coordinating Council for Women in History, the Association of Black Women Historians, the Berkshire Conference on the History of Women, the American Historical Association, the Organization of American Historians, the Latin American Studies Association, the Middle Eastern Studies Association, and many other conference groups that focus on specific areas of study. As noted earlier, the importance of joining these organizations and attending the gatherings and sessions for graduate students cannot be overemphasized. Contact information for these and other organizations can be found at http://www.theaha.org, http://www.oah.org, or http://www.h-net.msu.edu. These organizations usually offer reduced rates for students. For your dues, you will receive journals and newsletters that fill you in on new developments in scholarship and acquaint you with current issues in the profession. These publications also announce fellowships and upcoming conferences. Subscriptions to such associations' journals usually place your name on publishers' mailing lists. Publishers' catalogs will help keep you abreast of new publications.

PROFESSIONAL NETWORKING

Networking will broaden your professional horizons by exposing you to new situations and providing you with opportunities to meet historians in many different fields. It offers you a chance to look ahead into the world of historians to see how it appeals to you. If students are involved in your department's major committees, your participation may tell you a great deal about historians' values and expectations. The most educational experience is participation in a search committee's hunt for a new member of the department.

Attend departmental seminars, historical meetings in your region, and, if possible, national conventions. Meetings can yield immediate and long-term rewards even if they seem intimidating at first. The scheduled panels will give you a sense of what is expected when papers are presented and will help you plan to present a paper of your own. If you are an experienced conventioneer, you are less likely to be unnerved by the frenetic atmosphere at the convention where you may have your first job interview. Seek information about which associations are most likely to include student papers on their programs. (See Chapter 12 for more details.)

Don't let scheduled events at conferences absorb all your energy. The unscheduled opportunities to meet and exchange notes with people whose academic interests parallel your own are important advantages of going to professional meetings. This give-and-take can be personally and intellectually rewarding and may provide opportunities to offset the shortage or absence of role models for women graduate students, students of color, and gay and lesbian students. Meetings within the larger conference bring together articulate, dedicated, friendly scholars who share your interests and professional concerns. These smaller meetings will also provide a refuge. Remember that the bigger the convention, the more hectic the atmosphere will be. Scholars are also looking for other scholars. Don't feel ignored or discouraged when your conversations are brusque or cut short. It is important to make the effort to become part of the group.

INTERNATIONAL STUDENTS, STUDENTS OF COLOR, AND RETURNING STUDENTS

Everyone feels the stresses of graduate school, but international and returning students and students of color often feel particularly isolated. Attending a large public university with the opportunity to interact with other students inside or outside the classroom can be a very numbing experience for those who feel "different." You may feel left out of the normal student networks or departmental culture simply because you do not know the context of the discourse. For international students in particular, the strains of adjusting to a new society are exacerbated by a lack of social contact—many international students live on the fringes of graduate student circles until they complete their degrees, largely unnoticed by the larger circle of student colleagues, and sometimes even faculty, beyond their supervisory committee. Some international students and students of color are hesitant to seek redress for problems encountered, in some cases because they come from societies or cultures where the power imbalance between professor and student is large.

Again, you need not be gregarious to "network." Try to break through the isolation first by attending structured activities on campus. Both graduate history student associations and faculties organize regular brown bag lunch series and other seminars. Such events combine intellectual and social exchange and can be an important avenue for developing friendships. Wider graduate student social events can also be important icebreakers. In larger universities, you may also find colleagues from your country in various student clubs, some strictly social, others not. Does your university have an African students' association? A Latin American students' organization? Remember that various graduate student associations, including your history student group, can also provide support; they may help you to understand your rights as a student and keep you informed about professional associations and scholarly conferences.

If you are a returning student, you will, of course, be surrounded by younger colleagues fresh out of undergraduate school. If you have entered graduate school for personal development, not a career, try to keep the anxieties and ambitions of your younger colleagues in proper perspective. If you do intend to pursue an academic career, remember that you have as much right as any other student to do so and to tap into all the resources of your program.

More on the Returning Student

Students returning after a few—or many—years outside the academy will also face other unique hurdles. You have a more defined sense of self and are accustomed to a career and/or family life. Entering graduate school may have a different meaning for you than it has for younger peers. It is impossible to ignore family and other responsibilities in order to spend more time at a library or to do some last-minute work on a paper. A marked drop in your standard of living will follow if you give up a salary for graduate study.

Watch out for possible consequences of being out of the usual sequence in higher education. For example, women and men who enter graduate school directly after college arrive with study habits that you probably have long since discarded. Your priorities will shift as you make progress toward your degree. The first years of course work require organized commitments, often with little flexibility, and are followed by examinations and writing the dissertation— which allows you more independence in creating a schedule. It should get easier as you move toward your degree. Instead of seeing graduate work as one long continuing process, focus on it as a series of phases that will present different obligations and freedoms. The early years may be rigorously scheduled, but the expectations—attendance at classes and completion of papers—are clearly drawn. The later years provide flexibility but also require the ability to work independently.

Teachers are accustomed to students who exhibit typical student reflexes and outlooks. Instructors are sometimes younger than returning students and may treat you like other students, which can be disconcerting. The instructor's behavior may not be intentionally condescending, but it may appear that way to someone who has "lived in the adult world," and resentment may develop, taking the form of objecting to assignments or degree requirements. Beware of this psychological trap. Examine the situation objectively. Look for other faculty or students who can offer a better perspective on the situation. Above all, avoid convincing yourself that the parts of graduate training that you find irksome or inconvenient are simply obnoxious impositions. From time to time every department reviews its rules to adjust to changing realities, and the returning student can bring a fresh perspective to the process. Naturally, teachers find it easier to treat everyone alike rather than to develop a plan of study for each student. However, within the parameters of a sound education, teachers should tailor study to the student. A dialogue between older students and teachers may be a simple and direct solution.

Be careful, however, of asking for exemption from the usual rules on the grounds that your goals are different from those of other students. You may have entered the program only intending to satisfy an intellectual curiosity in a defined field and consequently regard a required historiography or quantitative methods course as an arbitrary hurdle. If you successfully petition for a waiver on this requirement, and then later develop ambitions for professional employment, you should not expect to be recommended along with those who have followed the plan of study established by the department.

Faculty Relationships

Get to know the faculty. You are planning to be a colleague someday, so it is reasonable to become familiar with faculty members. Faculty members expect more frequent dealings with graduate students than with undergraduates. See faculty members during office hours. Have your purpose clearly thought out and know how to end a conversation. You will be welcome for transactions of legitimate business and a certain amount of friendly conversation, but prolonged idle chitchat will put a strain on both of you. Do not overstay your welcome. Express your appreciation, then leave.

Some relationships with faculty will be particularly helpful to you, so pursue them. Seek out teachers who offer courses in your field. You should be able to respect them and to rely on them to recognize your successes but also to indicate your shortcomings. Faculty friends can give you personal reassurance and candid advice when needed.

Participate in seminars with faculty members from your department, other departments in the college, and outside speakers. Interdisciplinary seminars are often open to all interested scholars at any level. Watch how academics interact with one another. Learn what is considered a good seminar presentation, a good job talk, or a publishable paper. Gain as much insight as you can by watching and interacting with faculty in these settings.

You will need a faculty supervisor or advisor, or a team of supervisors, for your main field and the writing of your dissertation. The relationship between student and advisor takes many forms, primarily determined by the personality and pedagogical methods of the advisor. No matter what the individual approach to interacting with a student, the advisor's purpose is clear: to help you choose a subject, hear about your progress, make suggestions, speak for you if you want graduate assistantships or fellowships, help you revise drafts, and start the process of advertising you for career positions. If you get anything less you are being shortchanged. If you have a choice, it is wise to choose an advisor on the basis of what you know about the person's mentoring style in this vital relationship—always taking into account other pertinent considerations, such as academic fields or department restrictions.

A professor's sex, politics, age, or teaching style should not determine how that person relates to you and your work. Do not assume that younger or more casual faculty members will treat your work more sympathetically or less rigorously than anyone else will. Just because one professor allows you to use her first name when all the others expect more formal modes of address, for instance, does not mean that she will necessarily be more "laid back" or "easier" in her grading. The reverse may well be true. Women students in particular should avoid the pitfall of assuming that female and feminist faculty will automatically be their friends or allies. Most want to encourage women students, but your shared gender or feminist approach does not mean that you have a right to a privileged relationship. Faculty-student relationships, whether same or mixed gender, are complex.

As a junior colleague, you should treat all the faculty members in your department in a professional manner and expect to be treated in the same way. If, at any point, you are having serious doubts about the efficacy or appropriateness of your supervisory relationship, you may need to solicit advice from other trusted colleagues and/or the departmental supervisor about either approaching your advisor and discussing your concerns, or changing your supervisor entirely.

THE ISSUE OF SEXUAL HARASSMENT

When choosing an advisor, watch out for professors who are "friendly" in ways that will interfere with your education. For women there can be distinctive hazards in this regard, but there are generic concerns as well. Teachers who want hero worship or various kinds of psychological nourishment from their students often have trouble maintaining pedagogical rigor. Friendliness, of course, comes in healthier forms, and everyone appreciates it, but you should put scholarship first in your relationship with an advisor. Unfortunately, some professors will resort to sexual innuendo and harassment. This happens more often than one might think and is never to be tolerated.

Tap into the student network to find out where trouble may lie. Because relatively few sexual harassers are actually prosecuted, information on potential offenders may only be available through a campus grapevine. Tread with caution here and try to determine, from people you trust, what information is considered reliable.

Victims of sexual harassment, understandably, may prefer not to publicize their experiences, which makes later victims think they have encountered something highly unusual. Confused, ashamed, or even ambivalent about their own feelings, victims may try to pretend they are misreading the signals. Graduate students, relatively junior members of any university community, may worry that reporting sexual harassment by a superior, an undergraduate, or even another graduate student could jeopardize their careers or make them appear incompetent. These feelings are not unusual in such circumstances, so don't feel you have to deal with the problem on your own. A professional counselor can help you discern the situation. Ask for a referral from a friend, a local clinic, or a help hotline. Many campuses and communities fund such local resources. Difficult though it may be, you need to analyze what is going on and take action if you have grounds for complaint. If you are confused about what is going on you may want to confront the person directly. Often your forthright questioning will stop the offensive behavior. But if your efforts prove unavailing, don't be passive.

Sexual harassment is against the law, and is a form of sex discrimination. Unwelcome sexual advances, requests for sexual favors, and other verbal or physical conduct of a sexual nature constitute sexual harassment when it has the purpose or effect of unreasonably interfering with an individual's work performance or creates an intimidating, hostile, or offensive work environment. In an academic setting sexual harassment can be student-student, student-faculty, or employee-supervisor related. It can affect success in a course, the opportunity to take a course, dissertation advisement, promotion, hiring, fellowships, scholarships, salary increases, letters of recommendation, and working conditions. The American Historical Association's *Statement on Standards of Professional Conduct* and the National Council on Public History's "Ethical Guidelines for the Historian" address this very serious offense.

Most schools now have grievance procedures to handle sexual harassment cases. First, find out if your department has written guidelines concerning the issue. If not, it should. If you believe that you have been sexually harassed, seek help from appropriate sources immediately. Know your rights. There are ways of dealing with harassment short of bringing a lawsuit. You can let the harasser know unequivocally, in person or in writing, that the behavior is unwanted and uninvited. If you do this in writing, keep a copy and any proof that it was delivered to the harasser. Document each incident, including when and where it occurred, your response, who witnessed the incident, and whom you told. Keep a record of any letters, cards, or notes sent to you. Keep a record of your class work if relevant. Make a note of emotional or physical side effects, and document any medical consultations. Keep these materials in a safe place (not at work). A counselor in your school's human relations or affirmative action office may be able to advise you while keeping your identity confidential. File a formal complaint if your department or college has an internal complaint system. If this does not work, contact an attorney experienced in handling sexual harassment cases and begin to work through outside channels.

CHANGING PROGRAMS OR INSTITUTIONS

Despite the selection of the fields of study and examinations, regardless of the forethought you have given your choice, your plans may change in light of what you learn, your working environment and relationships, new opportunities, or personal interests or concerns. Interests based on undergraduate experiences often fade in graduate school. It is folly to stick with a subject you once loved if it becomes unbearably dreary.

If switching fields leads to a delay in acquiring languages or other skills, you may decide against such a change. The delay can be both long and expensive if, for example, you set out to master a non-European language. These extra burdens, however, are often worth it in the long run. Consult professors and other graduate students, of course, but remember that you alone can decide what to do.

At one time or another, discouragement and doubt strike most graduate students. Don't consider your own a sign of personal weakness or failure. Joyce Antler, commenting in "Personal Lives and Professional Careers: The Uneasy Balance" (Report of the Women's Committee of the American Studies Association), found that, according to a survey conducted in 1986, one of the most frequent personal problems faced by women academics is attitudinal, "characterized by self-doubt and guilt." According to the survey, women internalized blame for their perceived failure to meet their own professional or personal goals. This is a result of the privatization of academic stress and indicates the need for many more support systems for women and men at every phase of their careers. Try not to be overly influenced by these feelings if you can avoid it, but if you do, know that you are experiencing common human reactions to stress.

If you find that you are maltreated or find one program unsuitable, another may suit you better. You may have started out, for example, as a historian but soon discovered that contemporary social problems interest you more. See an academic advisor about switching departments or programs. Some credits you have accrued may be transferable. If a move is feasible, you might explore the possibility of changing universities. Such undertakings, however, whether among programs, departments, or universities, could be extremely costly. There is the risk of losing credits, and completion of the course of study may be delayed.

LEAVING THE PROFESSION

There is no point in subjecting yourself to more than a year of graduate school if you do not want to spend a good deal of your life working in the field of professional history. There are no laws that you must complete a degree just because you have started one.

If you are unsure of your motives for wanting a change, take a leave of absence for a year. Try working in a field that you think offers an alternative career. A year may be all you need to reach a conclusion about where your interests and talents lie.

Academic relationships are complex and constantly changing. The intellectual stimulation of a study group, the rewards of a good student-mentor relationship, the shared hopes and insights of students of all ages and backgrounds pursuing the common goals of higher education—these are the connections that foster growth and progress. Academic relationships are the foundation and support structures of a professional career.

❖ 5 ❖

FUNDING GRADUATE AND POSTDOCTORAL STUDY

MANY GRADUATE STUDENTS RECEIVE FUNDING TO HELP PAY FOR ALL OR PART OF their graduate education. In the best of cases, funding covers every year of course work for the MA or PhD and the dissertation stage. Funding is also available for postdoctoral study. Rarely, though, does all such funding come from the same source. It is important that you know both the phases of funding and how to apply for it.

ASSISTANTSHIPS

During your graduate study, it is possible your department will offer you part-time employment, whether in research, administration, or teaching. This offer may be made when you are first accepted into a program but more likely will come in your second or third year. The titles differ: graduate assistant, research associate, teaching fellow, or half-time lecturer, among others. Be sure you know what duties you will be expected to perform. All assistantships should be paid, have a stipulated number of hours per week, and have a predetermined work schedule for the semester. When you know the particulars, you can decide whether you want the job.

Pay for an assistantship will be meager. Everyone bemoans how low it is; nobody raises it much except to offset inflation. You may want to agitate for higher pay. If so, you have a strong claim. There are campuses where graduate students have unionized, drawing on relationships with other staff unions and affiliating with national union organizations. Unions representing graduate student employees have helped with tuition remittances, health care, grievance procedures, and similar concerns. Graduate students have had particular success organizing in their role as teachers. You might want to explore the possibility of joining or creating a union, although you will need to carefully balance your studies with your unionizing activities.

If you want an assistantship, apply early. Keep careful track of deadlines for applications and renewals. Get as much information as possible about how this process works. Your advisor should have up-to-date information about your progress and may be able to act as an advocate on your behalf to the assistantship committee if this is allowed in your school. In general, you will be judged on your successful graduate study and your aptitude for the work ahead. Assistantships are important. They not only provide financial assistance but also the development of teaching and research skills that future employers will want to see. The distribution of assistantships may also reflect a department's assessment of your future potential as a member of the profession.

Teaching Assistantships

Teaching assistantships are designed to provide you with teaching skills and afford you an opportunity to learn under professional guidance. Supervision decreases as your teaching experience increases. You often gain experience in courses outside your particular field. Most permanent teaching positions will require you to teach survey courses, and teaching assistantships can help prepare you for this. All teaching assistants (TAs) should be evaluated by both students and professors; their judgments will help you learn and, when the reports are good, will help you get a full-time job.

When you work as a TA in a course conducted by a full-time faculty member, that person is in charge of your professional conduct in that course. Therefore, that teacher may stipulate the assignments for your students in whole or in part, visit your classes, call on you to explain grades you assign or change them, or ask you to exchange papers for grading with another section assistant. The skillful supervisor will track your responsibilities, consult with you about improving the course, and conduct staff meetings where administrative details are cleared up quickly and the subject of the course is discussed.

Success as a teaching assistant can be extremely valuable when you look for a full-time teaching position. Everyone looks for evidence of pedagogical skills in candidates. It is greatly in your interest, therefore, to do well and to have faculty observers witness your triumphs in the classroom. Their comments, supported by student evaluations, will carry great weight. Still, being a TA has diminishing returns, especially if you are still only assisting the large survey courses. It is important to pursue opportunities to structure your own courses. And, if you have the choice between a teaching assistantship and a fellowship, you should remember that teaching always takes a great deal of time and can keep you from completing your dissertation.

RESEARCH ASSISTANTSHIPS

Research assistantships generally vary from teaching assistantships in that they build different skills and sometimes allow for more flexible work schedules. Students interested in public history jobs may prefer research assistantships. Their required tasks may range from working as a data gatherer and editor on a manuscript to data accumulation and cataloging for an archive. If possible, pursue a research assistantship at least once in your graduate years to help you build these practical historical skills. Discuss the opportunities available at your school or in your area with your advisor and, if possible, the directors of programs in museum studies or special public history projects.

FELLOWSHIPS AND GRANTS

Departments and colleges are not the only sources of funding for graduate studies, so do not rely solely on them for all your financial needs. As you move into the dissertation phase, begin gathering information about other funding sources. In some cases, fellowships or grants can be used to supplement department assistantships. MA students will also find information of interest.

There are many fellowships specifically targeted to graduate students. However, graduate students should consider themselves eligible for any grant directed at historical scholarship unless the granting agency specifically targets another audience (such as holders of the PhD) or indicates that graduate students are not eligible. While competition may be greater for these grants, they are not unattainable.

You should also consider applying for relevant research grants. There are grants aimed at all students, or all humanities and social science students, for which you can apply. While competition is stiff, they are not unattainable.

A WORD ABOUT FUNDING DECISIONS

Many students remain mystified by the process of how awards are granted. Professors from various universities sit on these committees. Some committees are composed entirely of professors from the same discipline. However, the recent trend is toward multidisciplinary committees whose members may be unaware of and indeed uninterested in the particular debates, jargon, and styles familiar to historians, but who are looking for important projects that have a wide appeal. In such competitions, the onus is on you to present your project with a nonspecialist audience in mind, to make your proposal accessible to non-historians, and to argue for the wider value, significance, or relevance of your work.

An important goal of funding is to reduce financial risk to the granting agency. Conscious of how little money there is to distribute, they put great weight on the reliability of references and proof of productivity. It may seem unfair, but a student who has already received one major award is more likely to receive other ones, because he or she is perceived as "successful." There are, of course, always exceptions. A well-written application for a strong project can win a fellowship based on merit and strategy.

PRELIMINARY INQUIRIES

Ask friends and former teachers about agencies to approach. Check out publications that list various grants and fellowships that are available. AHA members can access the regularly updated Grants Online at http://www.theaha.org/members.

Many universities now have a grants officer, whose duty it is to help faculty members write proposals for outside grants and fellowships. A grants officer will have material on hand from most funding agencies—application forms, statements of purpose, and the like—and experience in dealing with such agencies. The grants officer can help in many ways, such as calling the agency to clarify a question, or reading and commenting on your proposal. Don't assume, however, that the grants officer will know of all grants available to you. While grants officers attempt to be thorough, they also are usually responsible for covering many disciplines and may not be fully informed about all grants available to historians. If no such position exists at your university, you must go through the preliminary inquiries yourself.

If you are not sure if your project or qualifications will be judged suitable by a particular agency, write and ask. If there is any hint of requirements that would prejudice or prevent application because of race, sex, or age, press the agency further and notify the AHA Professional Division of the suspected discrimination at once.

When you write to an agency for an application, also ask for annual reports of the organization and the list of awards for the past several years. These can give you important clues that are not always specified in the fellowship brochure. The agency's policies can change as scholarly fields shift and as administrators come and go. The organization may concentrate grants regionally or prefer certain subjects or research methods. If such policies exist and suit you, fine. If not, write to find out if certain policies rule out your project. You may be saved the bother of applying.

FILING THE APPLICATION

Be sure to fill out the application form neatly and precisely. Stay within the recommended length, remembering that fellowship committees often have to read hundreds of applications. If you can, follow the style of a successful application; it can provide a helpful model. Some agencies accept preliminary proposals. If so, take advantage of this opportunity for help from agency staff.

Recognize your weaknesses as far as the agency is concerned, and emphasize your strengths on the application. Women in general, and older women especially, ought to emphasize their professional attitudes and commitment. This is best done not by direct assertion but by tone and statement of career plans. If your career shows unusual gaps that require explanation, like a period of withdrawal for family responsibilities or a paucity of research due to heavy teaching responsibilities, make a brief, straightforward statement of the facts with no apologies.

Choose people to write letters of recommendation or to referee your proposal who will strengthen your position. It is always wise to choose people who are clearly your senior in the field. If you are working in a subject that requires a variety of skills, try to get people who can testify to all needed attributes. If your career has been limited to a particular locale or to a wholly teaching-oriented institution, try to include a recommendation from someone in a nationally recognized department, even if that person is familiar only with an earlier stage of your career. It is almost always useful to get letters of recommendation from people outside your home institution.

If submission of supporting materials is permitted, these may be helpful, but don't send very long papers. If you must, add an abstract indicating which sections show the heart of your work.

If a budget is required as part of the application, be as realistic as possible in estimating your needs. As important as the total amount of money requested is the rationale, so add a note explaining your reasoning in constructing the budget. Agencies differ on such requirements, and it is wise to seek the advice of someone who is well informed about a particular agency.

THE PROJECT STATEMENT

Your statement of the project should be oriented to each individual agency. Most subjects have many dimensions, and it is entirely appropriate to emphasize the area in which each agency is particularly interested. For example, if you want to write a biography of Elizabeth Blackwell, you might stress to the Rockefeller Program in Women's Studies how your book will add to the understanding of women in the nineteenth century; to the National Institutes of Health Program in the History of Medicine you can relate your study to the history of medical practice; to the Social Science Research Council you can show how Blackwell illuminates problems of professionalization and gender roles; to the National Endowment for the Humanities you might emphasize the variety of topics Blackwell's life and work spanned and your intent to relate her accomplishments to a wider audience. You cannot, of course, claim to do all these things unless you really intend to. But the process of applying for fellowships should lead you to discover the richness of your own subject and to think systematically about how to bring it out.

Your project statement should focus on the questions and issues it addresses, not on a narrative statement of the subject. A biography, for instance, is a traditional form that in itself would hold little appeal for fellowship agencies. Yet a biography can be presented—as it should be conceived—as a case study in various historical problems. This also applies to other topics. Any subject gains interest from a sharp focus on relevant historical issues.

This focus will help you make the strongest possible case for your project's importance. Even if such a statement is not required, be sure to show how your project adds to what is already known, explores new methods, or makes new materials available.

Finally, it is very important to have several other people read your proposal before you submit it. Someone well versed in your field can make useful suggestions. So can a person outside the field, since things that seem clear to members of the field can mystify others. Some agencies ask you to send the proposal to a referee who then comments on the project as well as your capabilities. In that case, send it to the referee well in advance of the deadline. In addition to asking for a judgment on a recommendation, ask how the proposal might be improved. In general, be sure someone well informed looks over the completed application, including budget and career statements as well as the prospectus of your project. Exchanging information and advice is a professional duty. Don't hesitate to ask for help.

REAPPLYING

If you fail to get the fellowship, do not be content with a form letter of rejection. Write and ask for advice and particulars. Would it be worthwhile to apply again next year? Is there a weakness in the application that you might strengthen? Private foundations may not respond, but government agencies are now required to summarize evaluations for those who request it. Don't give up after one year's try. Many chance circumstances enter into a decision and you could succeed next time.

OTHER EMPLOYMENT, INTERNSHIPS, AND VOLUNTEER WORK

Many graduate students maintain some form of employment alongside their studies, including quite a few with part-time employment teaching at other institutions. Part-time teaching, summer jobs, internships, and volunteer work can provide you with opportunities to test your interest in a variety of fields. Internships are available with local, state, or federal agencies; foundations; newspapers and other media organizations; public interest groups; and other professions. Some pay well. All give you a chance to develop skills not cultivated in graduate school. After completing an internship, you may decide you would rather work as a historian with a state government than teach, or perhaps you would prefer to leave the profession and become a journalist. *Careers for Students of History*, a pamphlet updated in 2002 by the American Historical Association and the National Council on Public History, covers a broad range of occupations for historians. It includes information on internships, summer and volunteer jobs, and helpful publications issued by professional organizations.

Temporary jobs will give you a new perspective on academic work. They will also look good on your record when you seek long-term employment, particularly if the positions are history related. Historic preservation work, editing, archival research, or apprenticeships at museums are all areas that indicate a serious professional interest in history and demonstrate your willingness to develop skills beyond the usual graduate school offerings. Part-time work also can provide job contacts or a lucrative way to help finance your dissertation. Most importantly, participation in professional activities will encourage you to take yourself seriously as a scholar—perhaps the most important element for success in graduate school and professional self-definition.

Those employed in teaching are further developing crucial job skills, but the many others in less applicable employment should not to be too discouraged at the necessity of taking on other jobs. This too can have its own rewards.

Assistantships, grants, and fellowships provide more than financial support. They also give you and your projects prestige. Use these awards as building blocks to more grants or jobs. Their long-term benefits are as important as their short-term rewards of skills and money.

❖ 6 ❖

THE JOB SEARCH

DEFINING GOALS

IT'S TIME TO INITIATE YOUR FIRST REAL JOB SEARCH. THE CURRENT EMPLOYMENT market for academic historians is not very encouraging. A recent increase in retirements of tenured faculty at universities has not produced the almost unlimited opportunities that were predicted a decade ago. Even though many new jobs are being created, because of the difficulties in the job market of the mid- to late 1990s there are many applicants for each open position. At the same time, a number of universities have been replacing tenure-track positions with part-time and temporary employees. Nevertheless, you must approach the job market with a positive attitude and with the skills to land a good position.

Be realistic about your prospects. Unless you hold a master's degree in a specialty that does not require additional study, you will find fewer doors open to you. For most professional positions—and certainly for any prospect of long-term employment in the academy—the doctorate is needed, so do not pursue such positions until the PhD is clearly in sight.

Be wary of financial pressures that may lead you to rush into an academic job. You may find that finishing a dissertation while otherwise employed takes longer than your employer is willing to wait. Even if you finish the dissertation and are able to keep your job for a few more years, you may not be able to put the effort into publishing sufficiently to qualify for a longer term. In institutions following American Association of University Professors guidelines, faculty members are allowed six years to qualify for tenure. That may sound like a long time, but it will pass quickly under the demands of teaching and publishers' deadlines.

Don't assume that you must stay in the academic world as a professor. Museums and historical societies are increasingly seeking historians with PhDs, so do not rule out these positions. There are numerous benefits to employment outside the academy—no tenure stress, the ability to communicate with diverse audiences and kindle respect for history and the work of historians, greater (in some instances) promotional opportunities, and less need to pack up and relocate. If you want to consider this option, you may wish to do an internship in a museum, seek work consulting on a museum exhibit, or get involved in state humanities programming; any of these activities will help you understand the challenges of presenting history to a broad public audience.

CAREER AND PLACEMENT OFFICE SERVICES

If you are interested in non-academic jobs, you can probably find help at your school's career or placement office. Visit your placement office early and often to find out about funding and job opportunities. The career office will help you look into these possibilities. Students can usually attend orientation seminars and schedule individual appointments with a career counselor. Career counselors assist students by developing individualized career plans, discussing career alternatives, refining job-seeking skills, and providing job placement assistance.

Whether you are seeking academic employment or not, the most important service of the career office is its credentials service. Students' academic and professional recommendations are kept on file and may be used for employment, admissions, and postgraduate fellowship purposes.

The placement office should have all the appropriate forms. Your file or dossier should contain a transcript of your graduate school grades, a curriculum vitae (c.v.) or resumé on a form used by the placement office, and reference letters.

THE PROFESSIONAL DOSSIER

Particularly when seeking academic employment, a c.v. should show the extent of your training and experience in the historical profession. Be sure to include basic information: name, address, telephone numbers (both home and office numbers), e-mail address, and citizenship.

While you can simply photocopy your c.v. or run off a copy on a computer, using a high-quality white or ivory rag or bond paper looks more professional, and tends to make it stand out in a large stack of c.v.'s on standard white paper. A good source of information on resumé writing for historians is available from the Organization of American Historians in *From Job Crisis to Job Opportunities: The OAH/FIPSE Project Careers Packet*. After listing the basic information, detail your professional education. List all degrees from BA on, but go into detail only on graduate study: fields, subject, dissertation supervisor, and other major research projects. List any honors and fellowships. Mention teaching assistantships or comparable preparation for employment.

List professional positions, most recent first, beginning with your current job. Give titles and stipulate whether the jobs were part or full time. Opinions differ on whether to account for gaps in employment or education. Some prefer to leave them unexplained and let prospective employers ask about them. Women or men who have interrupted a career to raise a family may want to mention it in the dossier or in the accompanying cover letter. Regardless of how you treat any gaps, make clear how you kept professional skills polished during these intervals—by keeping abreast of publications, writing articles, attending professional meetings, and so forth.

Next, list your publications and public presentations of papers and commentary. The further you are in your career, the more selective you can get. Beginners are wise to note anything that shows active participation in the profession.

The status of a book or article that is in the publication pipeline is often an important piece of information to a search committee or fellowship review committee. Yet the profession has no standardized terminology, often rendering that status unclear. The AHA suggests the following lexicon.

- "In Press": The publication is out of the author's hands. It lies somewhere in the production process.
- "Forthcoming": A press or journal has accepted the publication. Author is making final revisions to a completed text.
- "Under Contract to…": A press and an author have signed a contract for a book in progress.
- "Submitted" or "Under Consideration": The book or article has been submitted to a press or journal.

Describe the work you are prepared to do—what subjects you are ready to teach or what other tasks you are trained for. A syllabus backs this up. Prepare a statement on your teaching philosophy.

Give a brief description of your current research, how you are revising your dissertation, and maybe a prediction of what you might work on next. If you anticipate further training, mention that.

Keep dossiers up-to-date and always have a supply of copies of your c.v. available. As your experiences accumulate, revise the basic c.v. to include your progress. Drop references that pertain only to your earliest years in graduate study and add letters from people who have a fresh understanding of your work. A common error is leaving in an outdated letter. For instance, when you have completed your dissertation, ask your advisor to write a new letter that fully evaluates what you've accomplished.

WHERE TO FIND JOB LISTINGS

Once you have decided on the positions you would like to pursue and assessed your skills, use every possible avenue to track down employment opportunities. To search for a job, turn to teachers, the department's placement officer, the college placement office, professional journal and newspaper ads, and your own initiative. For teaching positions, consult the Employment Information section of the AHA's monthly newsletter, *Perspectives*, which can be found online at www.theaha.org; H-Net at www.matrix.msu.edu/jobs/; the *Chronicle of Higher Education*, published weekly, at www.chronicle.com; and selected publications in your field. The *Affirmative Action Register* is directed at women, minorities, veterans, and the physically disabled and should be consulted for administrative, managerial, and professional positions. Interdisciplinary listings can be found in the American Studies Association *Newsletter*. Some departments receive subscriptions to these publications. If your department does not, urge the administrator to sign up.

JOBS FOR PUBLIC HISTORIANS

Much of the information regarding employment in colleges and universities is relevant to historians working in museums, archives, government, or state and local historical societies. However, because these positions are located in more diverse institutions, it is essential to become familiar with the structure and policies of the organization in which you are seeking employment. State and federal agencies operate under civil service rules for retention and promotion. In private agencies, the board of directors may be the ultimate arbiter of hiring, evaluation, and promotion practices. In some cases, public programs or your own salary may depend on your ability to raise funds.

Public historians have the ability to reach new audiences with historical work and to educate general audiences in historical inquiry and methods. By maintaining an active presence at professional meetings, public historians can do much to educate their colleagues about the promotion of historical knowledge in this larger field. By pursuing their own scholarship and enlisting academic historians as consultants and colleagues, public historians can counter the insularity that sometimes plagues their own agencies.

For public history positions, consult publications of other professional associations in addition to *Perspectives*. The AHA's *Directory of History Departments, Historical Organizations, and Historians* lists more than 1,000 public historians, employed in a wide variety of areas and fields. If you are in an archival training program, see *American Archivist*, published by the Society of American Archivists, and consult the *Newsletter*. For museum jobs, see *Aviso*, published by the American Association of Museums, and the newsletter of the American Association for State and Local History. Many public history jobs are advertised only on the local level, so those interested should be sure to check the employment listings in local newspapers, many of which are now available through the World Wide Web.

The federal government provides many opportunities for those seeking public history employment. Federal agencies frequently have their own historical programs; the Department of Defense, for example, has a particularly large staff of military historians. The National Archives and the National Park Service are also major employers of historians, and there are many historians at the State Department.

Unfortunately, there is no reliable central source of information concerning openings for federal jobs. Each federal agency has its own personnel office (sometimes more than one) and you will need to contact each agency individually. A look at the annual *United States Government Manual* (found online at http://www.access.gpo.gov/nara/nara001.html) will help you choose the agencies or committees where you might like to work. The Society for History in the Federal Government regularly publishes a *Directory of Federal Historical Programs and Activities*, a listing of federal offices with historians, which is available from the AHA. If you are interested in a particular department, contact that agency's staff historian. Job listings are also available through the World Wide Web at http://www.usajobs.opm.gov/ and http://www.fedworld.gov/jobs /jobsearch.html. Federal agencies also advertise in publications such as *Perspectives* or the *Chronicle of Higher Education*. For positions in the nation's capital, see the *Washington Post* classifieds.

Consider a variety of issues before deciding when to first seek an academic position. Positive feedback on your work at conferences or with respect to a publication may encourage you to try your luck, or your economic circumstances might necessitate a search for a temporary or part-time job. On the other hand, the job market in your area might be quite dismal at the moment, or your supervisor may discourage you from applying for positions in the belief that such a move is premature and/or will hamper your progress toward thesis writing. Teaching experience is desirable in the current job market, but do not assume that sessional or part-time teaching will inevitably lead to a tenure-track position. There seems to be a limit of perhaps five years for adjunct work before it damages a tenure job hunt. And keep in mind that teaching positions are labor and time intensive and will slow down the progress of your own work, perhaps considerably delaying the completion of your dissertation. Of course, you may be constrained by your need to bring in a living income; financial pressures may push you into looking for part- or even full-time academic work prior to finishing your thesis. Still, ponder your situation and options carefully. You may wish to consider temporary employment outside of academe (if it is available) so you have more time for your own writing, rather than spending a large amount of time in a possibly underpaid sessional job. If you are not under extreme financial pressure, you should ask yourself if a time-consuming teaching position is worth delaying the completion of your thesis and possibly decreasing your appeal as a candidate for a permanent position.

❖ 7 ❖

SURVIVAL AT INTERVIEWS

SUCCESSFUL ACADEMIC INTERVIEWING

THE FOLLOWING DISCUSSION IS DIRECTED BOTH TO INTERVIEWERS AND candidates and assumes that both have mutual interests. Ideally, both want to exchange as much accurate and relevant information as possible about the qualities and credentials of the candidate and the nature of the job. Yet both face temptations that can lead to unproductive interviews. One temptation for the interviewer is created by the fact that the interview often constitutes an occasion for conversing with colleagues; these occasions are unfortunately rare, especially in big departments. It is always satisfying to discover how interesting our departmental colleagues are, but such discussions unfortunately detract from the interview process. A related problem arises when interviewers want to demonstrate their own erudition. Interviewees frequently face the problem that their anxiety and desire not to offend suppress their natural personality and make them appear less interesting than they actually are. Thorough planning and preparation for the interview will make such mistakes less likely.

Inadequate preparation on both sides is a very common mistake and often results from denying that good interviewing requires a lot of work on both sides. Candidates must be prepared to face search committees who have not read their material and to present condensed descriptions of their work to other department members who may not have even read the accompanying c.v. If the interviewer does not know the candidate's work, important questions may not emerge until the candidate has left. Candidates can try to refocus a wandering interview by emphasizing their recent work.

Candidates should not hesitate to send ahead any *reasonable* amount of material, even beyond what is requested, to strengthen their case: the goal is to make one's work known. Candidates should also study a prospective department's makeup. Are women and minorities well represented? Do faculty members represent more than one age group? What are the areas of strength and research interests among the faculty? Candidates might find it useful to read (or at least look at) the work of department members. Interviewers reasonably interpret this knowledge or lack of it as evidence of interest and sophistication.

CONVENTION INTERVIEWS

Prior to a convention interview, the hiring institution should announce job specifications as clearly as possible, and also should announce ways to locate the interviewers at the convention. At large conventions such as the American Historical Association's annual meeting, recruiters often are not assigned hotel rooms in advance of registration and the efficiency of mail and phone message systems varies from hotel to hotel. To ensure that candidates can easily find pre-arranged interviews, search committees should enter their names and hotel numbers as soon as possible in the locator system at the Job Register, and check for e-mails at the messaging system.

There are conflicting opinions about whether or not to attend a convention without a prescheduled interview. If you think it will be worthwhile, go ahead. Remember, though, that you will be responsible for all your expenses for the trip, and the money might be better spent pursuing job possibilities in other ways. Less than a third of the search committees interviewing at the annual meeting will be accepting c.v.'s, so you should adjust your expectations accordingly. Even if you have prearranged interviews scheduled, you need to be realistic. Search committees typically use the annual meeting job register only for preliminary interviews; candidates who attend expecting a job offer at the end may be sorely disappointed.

Interviews conducted at conventions are grueling situations for everyone, because many candidates are interviewed in quick succession. The interview should illuminate what is unique about each candidate, but to do this both sides must necessarily repeat themselves. The candidate should be able to provide capsule summaries of the dissertation or other current work, preferably in two versions: one in less than five minutes, one a bit longer. Each version should begin with a summary of main arguments (not just a description of the topic) and should at least hint at, if not cover, sources, theoretical content, and what is new and important about the work. Many young scholars have difficulty in asserting the importance of their work and construe their research in the most insignificant terms possible. Avoid beginning the summary apologetically or negatively by describing what is omitted or what the work does not do. Do not be so cautious that you refuse to think and talk beyond the limits of the dissertation. Be prepared to talk about how your work will or should influence future scholarship in various areas. Be prepared to answer the question, "So what?"

Interviewers will find it useful to draw out the candidates' views of their dissertations in order to get an opportunity to see how candidates handle a historical argument and what relationships exist between conclusion and evidence; these are tests of the candidates' qualities of mind. Interviewers often ask candidates for perspectives on the general development of the field (say, colonial American history) in the past decade or two: Can candidates identify the big historiographical patterns? Do they know the literature outside their dissertation topic?

Candidates should also be prepared to discuss a long-term research agenda—if possible, a project beyond the dissertation—or, at a minimum, a vision of how the dissertation will be revised. Candidates should consider carefully whether to present themselves as continuing the same topic or ranging further. If this question is not posed, find ways of introducing it. You may have difficulty setting the agenda and seizing the conversational initiative. Bolster your courage in advance, perhaps by asking friends to participate in a mock interview by posing some difficult questions. You can also participate in practice sessions held each year at the AHA annual meeting.

Although the hierarchical nature of academia, combined with social inequalities in the academy and the wider world, may seem to require attitudes of deference, such behavior does not usually produce good interviews. Confidence is almost always an asset. This does not mean bragging or listing all your honors; real confidence is reflected in a willingness to offer genuine opinions and to respond to thought-provoking questions.

You should also take into account the type of institution you are applying to. Interviewing for a position at a small undergraduate college will call for a different emphasis. Typically today's non-elite small undergraduate colleges need broadly trained historian-teachers who think an intellectual challenge is learning new fields and doing comparative non-Western and world history. In fact, there is a good chance you will eventually be called upon to teach outside the discipline itself. If candidates sound too committed to their narrow field, they may never get to an on-campus interview. A small-college professor afraid to take on new areas and broad intellectual challenges can become more of a departmental "paperweight" than a worthwhile colleague.

For small colleges, hiring decisions can have serious personal and professional repercussions. Successful new faculty can bring positive recognition to a department of any size, but the reality is that any one assistant professor in a large program has relatively little impact on the lives and careers of his or her colleagues. A failed assistant professor in a large department is merely one of 20 or 30 members. On the other hand, in a small department such failure can potentially destroy the program, driving away majors and killing otherwise popular courses.

PREPARING FOR ON-CAMPUS INTERVIEWS

The more carefully planned, the better the campus visit. Search committee chairs should have detailed schedules, preferably in writing, for candidates' visits. These should include rest breaks. It is helpful to find guestrooms as near as possible to the center of activity so that candidates can retire for an hour if they like. Because junior candidates may find it difficult to ask assertive questions, interviewers should provide information about the schedule and procedure for hiring decisions, how many candidates are being interviewed, and what the prospects and requirements are for tenure. Interviewers should keep questions exclusively to professional matters, and should, whenever possible, include women and minority faculty among the interviewers.

The candidates in turn should ask for detailed information about the interview procedure. Don't hesitate to ask very specific questions: What will the schedule be like (hour by hour if possible)? Where will you stay overnight? Whom will you see? If you are giving a talk, ask the size of the audience, the type of room, the makeup of the audience (whether it will be largely students, largely faculty, or open to the public), and exactly how long the talk is expected to be.

Candidates should beware of the following: Many interviewers try to set candidates at ease by emphasizing the informality of the interview. Take these assurances with a large grain of salt. You are better off sticking to generally observed formalities. This means, for example, that if a talk is expected, bring a written paper. Of course, the degree of formality may vary from place to place; question your hosts closely.

Be very certain that your talk is the right length, the right volume, and is delivered with minimal repetitive mannerisms. If possible, practice in front of friends. Be prepared to answer any questions concisely.

Above all, present your strongest possible material. See that your presentation of your research hits all the scholarly requirements—particularly a clear argument, good use of (preferably original) sources, critical standards of evidence, awareness of other relevant scholarship (particularly that written by members of the department), and is an inherently interesting and, if possible, important topic. Tie your research to your teaching interests and philosophy.

The specifics of a dress code are more problematic for women than for men, but they can be exaggerated. Academics in general (at least outside New York, and with other striking exceptions) are not as sensitive to dress codes as many other professionals. It is appropriate to think "conservative." But in academia it does not appear to be necessary to dress like a Wall Street broker. Be prepared to walk, as the distances across campuses can be great.

Comments about your appearance can be unnerving. If someone compliments you on your looks, you may wish to acknowledge it with a smile or a nod and promptly change the subject. If that fails, you can say that you would feel more comfortable concentrating on your academic credentials. If there is an implied insult, you may need to challenge it directly, although if you still want the job you may wish to help the interviewer save face. You might try to defuse the tension with humor, or simply ignore it and try to move on. Remember the interview process is stressful for both parties; it may be that no offense was intended.

Once on campus, candidates are likely to have a series of brief meetings with individuals and small groups of faculty that will require repetitive descriptions of work and background. There will often be an interview with a dean. Be prepared to discuss the particulars of each section of your dissertation: research problems and how you solved them, new sources discovered, and anecdotes from within the dissertation.

Be prepared to ask questions about the department and campus. Think about this in advance to avoid repeating the basics. Candidates should certainly inquire about the following: teaching load, research support, leave time, enrollments, promotions and evaluation procedures, department structure, anticipated hirings, and library facilities. Try to ask about basic issues and problems that all colleges have, such as: Is the school well funded? Are salary increases made regularly? Is the department congenial or factionalized? Is there much interdisciplinary work for students or faculty? It is also useful to ask about the community—its resources, schools if you have children, housing, etc. These questions can be asked without overconfidence, as if you were certain of getting the job offer (see Appendix A, "A Checklist of Job Interview Queries," which covers a broad range of pertinent issues).

Women and minorities should direct special energy toward other women and minorities in the department. Their state of mind may tell you about conditions for women and minorities at this campus, although you should consider asking the interviewer directly about the status of women and minorities on the faculty. Candidates who ignore female and minority faculty do so at their peril. The fact that women and minorities have a harder time getting jobs and promotions does not mean they're not respected once in faculty positions, and their opinions may count for a lot.

Handling innocent questions about your personal situation can usually be done through a certain degree of tact. But there are no simple or easy answers for dealing with overt sexism, racism, and/or homophobia in the interview process itself. In considering your response to offensive comments you will have to weigh various factors: Is the entire department pervaded by a sexist/racist/homophobic culture (in which case you will have to ask yourself whether you want to become a part of such a department at all) or is it limited to a few individuals? Are you confident enough to challenge such comments directly at the interview, or would it be better to let them slip by and address the problem later, after a final hiring decision has been made?

It is entirely up to you as to how to deal with probing or offhand questions or remarks about your personal life. Feel free to discuss your situation if you like, but plan responses in advance if you wish to retain your privacy. You can always state simply that you have no personal commitments that would prevent you from taking the position. You will have to assess each situation as it arises and respond in a manner that you are personally comfortable with. On the other hand, don't feel that you must converse only about professional topics; it is useful and important to let people know about your other interests in life. Indeed, letting your interviewers know about what sort of things you like doing in your spare time (such as collecting antiques, volunteer social or political work, watching and playing sports) is an important means for them to get to know you as a potential colleague.

No amount of good advice can obviate the fact that interviews are full of arbitrary, capricious interactions and unexpected events. Interviewees will make mistakes, but a good interviewer can distinguish them from incompetence, so you need not think you must be perfect. Moreover, some of the best interviews will deviate from the rules and will exhibit some human oddities but will still honor the spirit and purpose of the event: to focus on the academic skills of the candidate.

Whether or not you are the top candidate, you may find the chair or someone else drawing you into a practical discussion about your interest in this job and your requirements. Do not be misled—the same discussion may be had with all interviewees. Don't hesitate to ask about what the job offer might include, but this is not a good time to make special demands that might accord you privileges above other department members, such as a lower teaching load or leave time. If you have other interviews, be sure to let them know this, but do not exaggerate.

You may also be a participant in many social occasions from breakfast through evening cocktails. Don't be fooled: These are never simply social occasions; you are always being interviewed. You might wish to avoid drinking alcohol. Interviewers may use these occasions to fish for information about your personal or family circumstances. As noted above, you should respond to such questions with caution if you want to retain your privacy. Don't hesitate to ask for small breaks (before your talk or between appointments) or to retire if you feel exhausted and need to go to sleep early. Interviewers often empathize with the strain and should be expected to sympathize with your need for a break or rest.

OTHER TIPS FOR ACADEMIC INTERVIEWS

Find out if the institution attaches non-academic rules to faculty positions. There may be codes of deportment that the faculty must observe or creeds they must support or subscribe to, particularly among church-related institutions. You will be told about the latitude of permissible beliefs but perhaps not about other aspects of campus life that you may find you cannot live with.

Graduate students often sit on search committees. The student's status is not necessarily announced. Find out if one of the interviewers is a graduate student, then follow up with specific questions or comments about matters of concern to graduate students at the university. If graduate students from the department are not on the search committee at a convention, they may still be attending the conference, so arrangements may be made for a separate meeting. Use the locator file or electronic message system to set up a time to meet. This may be a good way to find out about the graduate students' views of the department.

A host department will usually reimburse your expenses for visiting the campus, but whatever the arrangements, be sure they are clear in advance. Some institutions offer little or no financial help to candidates for interviews. Such institutions may invite a large number of applicants for campus visits. On the whole, if the interview is to be mostly at your expense, your chances of getting the job are diminished. In the better case, when your way will be paid, you will be expected to provide receipts for all major expenditures. Supply your Social Security number; quite a few schools need it before they can reimburse you. Normally schools will reimburse you later, rather than pay for your transportation in advance.

You have one more obligation after the interview is completed. Make sure you thank the interviewers immediately. Within a day or two of your meeting, send a letter to the chair of the search committee and to the graduate students if a separate meeting was arranged. Use appropriate business style and high-quality paper. This is your chance to emphasize or expand on how you are extremely qualified for the job and how the department would benefit by hiring you. Thank the interviewer for spending time with you.

INTERVIEWING AT ARCHIVES, HISTORICAL SOCIETIES, AND MUSEUMS

The rituals and routines of professional hiring off-campus are less codified than interviews for faculty positions, but the basic objectives are similar. The interviewers want to get to know you and your abilities, and you want to know more about the prospective position and work environment. Be aware that interviewers may perceive university-based historians as somewhat insular; therefore you should show that you have thought about the special demands and rewards of doing historical work that reaches beyond a scholarly audience. Interviewers are likely to be looking for someone with a genuine interest in their constituency, whether it is the museum-going public, the research-oriented clientele of an archive, or the supporting agency itself, such as the U.S. Senate Historical Office or the Federal Judicial Center. Find out about the structure and funding of the institution and its projects.

Interviewees should be aware that the daily routines, expectations, and resources of such positions vary greatly. In a small museum with a modest budget, you may be responsible for raising money, planning programs, and designing and hanging exhibits, as well as providing historical expertise. In a large agency, you may carry out specific duties on a daily basis and also get the opportunity to initiate your own special projects. You should ask about issues such as travel money, support for research, leave time, and the like. Some positions offer little or no time for individual research; others consider such work an integral part of professional advancement. At the same time, beware of focusing only on the perquisites. Just as university search committees would look askance at a candidate who appeared uninterested in teaching, so, too, are museums, archives, and agencies reluctant to hire someone who may want only to be seen as a future scholar-in-residence. You must focus on how your skills and interests fit the central work of the institution.

Awaiting a Response

When you leave an interview, the interviewers usually thank you for your time and say they have learned a lot from talking with you. Don't expect to be offered a job on the spot. This only happens on the rarest occasions.

Most interviewers will inform you when they have made a selection, but practice differs as to when the word is sent. Some schools will tell you as soon as they have taken you off the list. That ends the suspense and many candidates are grateful for the small relief. Other schools think it kinder to say nothing until they have made an offer that has been accepted or until the search has been given up for some reason. A letter reporting the result is then sent to all who have been interested in the position. This procedure avoids offending those who have been ruled out early. It assures the candidates that the position actually has been filled, abolished, or may be filled after a further search. Candidates are also entitled to ask for reasons why they were taken off the list. Keep in mind, though, that the answers may be less than satisfactory because they are phrased to avoid giving occasion for further inquiry or lawsuit; however, they may be helpful guides for future interviews. Candidates should also feel free to ask for immediate notification if they are eliminated from the list of prospects and should expect some kind of word sooner or later. Above all, anyone who has been invited for an on-campus interview and then removed from the list has a right to hear about the decision. Rejection is not easy, but there are other issues at stake besides you and your qualifications. A department hires around its current weaknesses and to build on its strengths. Also, new PhDs should be aware that they are in competition with people who have more experience.

A final note regarding job searches in any sector, public or private: If you know that you would not take a certain job, because of its location or for another reason, drop it from your list. Don't apply for jobs you are not ready to consider seriously. However, give yourself a fair chance—a situation may look more attractive once you've seen it close up.

❖ 8 ❖

CONSIDERING AND ACCEPTING JOB OFFERS

HOW THE JOB OFFER IS PRESENTED

A VERBAL OFFER MADE BY THE DEPARTMENT HEAD, IN PERSON OR ON THE telephone, should be followed by a written offer, stipulating rank, salary, teaching load, and other information. Do not consider yourself officially hired, resign your current position, or withdraw yourself from consideration in other searches until you have received and replied to a written offer. You should be allowed a reasonable amount of time to make your decision (in the case of an assistant professorship, usually a week). If the letter states a condition such as "This offer requires the ultimate approval of the President and Trustees," the tender may be withdrawn even after you accept. Act circumspectly. The institution may want to maintain its discretionary powers of veto, particularly because of budgetary considerations, while department chairs and deans want to treat the hiring as settled even if they have acted without final approval. When conditions of hiring have been disputed in court, the decisions handed down have been inconsistent. If possible, stay on the safe side; wait for approval of the offer in writing by the institution's final authority.

THE FORMAL CONTRACT

Some institutions do not use formal contracts, so it is wise to be clear on this point as soon as an offer is made. The letter offering the position and your reply accepting it may constitute the contract where no further document is used. It is important to be satisfied that this letter contains all the specifications that have been made during the final interview. For instance, if this is a tenure-track position, you must have an explicit statement to that effect. If the institution uses formal contracts, presentation of the document for your signature may be delayed until shortly before the academic year. Be sure of the document's contents; the agreement must be made in writing with the corroboration of responsible officials—dean, department head, or whoever has the authoritative word—on what the contract will contain when it is tendered to you.

In the case of public history positions, be sure to find out in advance if restrictions concerning publications or consulting are acceptable to you. Some jobs may require prior clearance of all publications, even if written freelance. Some agencies have conflict-of-interest rules that may prevent you from engaging in work you want to do on your own time.

CONTRACT NEGOTIATIONS

When an offer is made, in whatever form, it should include precise language on how long the offer will remain in effect—that is, how much time you have to accept it, turn it down, or negotiate revision. Do not be intimidated by the idea of negotiation. It is expected that some negotiation will take place.

Significant revision can be difficult, especially for first-year faculty. You must be extremely alert to all nuances if you intend to negotiate. Your leverage is that the department wants you and wants you to be happy. How far can you push? Do you have a strong case for what you want? Determine these aspects by comparing your situation to similar cases of other new colleagues, if possible, and by how those at the other end of the negotiation table respond to you.

MAKING THE DECISION

If you get an offer and you think other schools may be about to approach you, inform the other institutions of the current offer, indicating the time within which you must respond. If other institutions want to compete for your services, they may do so, but do not count on this happening.

Your decision should be based on the realization that the job you choose will play a central role in your life for some time. Evaluate the offer fairly. If you are unsure of any information, contact the department and confirm details. Don't let money cloud the decision-making process. Don't accept one job simply because the starting salary is a few thousand dollars more. Think about future advancement, tenure prospects, living and social environment, and other matters. Look at support services, class size, teaching opportunities, sabbatical rules, and benefits packages. Discuss the job offer with family, friends, and colleagues, but trust your own judgment.

After you have accepted a position, it is courteous to write to other institutions that you know have been seriously considering you to tell them of your decision.

PART-TIME OR SHORT-TERM POSITIONS

Part-time teaching can mean many things. You could be appointed to a part-time adjunct line, teaching one or more courses, or you could accept a one- to three-year appointment. These positions will provide you with teaching experience while you are still in graduate school or with employment in the profession while you are applying for more permanent jobs. Some historians also take on adjunct or other part-time teaching to hone their skills while holding other professional positions, such as curatorships.

Grants and funding for limited-duration employment ("soft money") provide another form of short-term work for historians, allowing many historians to work in the field on special projects for a specified length of time. Some historians have chosen this route to allow for more independence in research and writing.

There are many positive aspects of part-time and short-term work. These options permit involvement in the professional environment without many of the attendant responsibilities of full-time work. It can help to advance long-term goals, especially for beginning historians who cannot yet take on full-time teaching or research jobs because they are still in school. But there are also negative aspects of this type of work. Part-time positions offer schools cheap labor and help them fill situations in an emergency. Most positions lack benefits unless, for example, one is an adjunct for ten years at the same school. This varies, of course, but individuals should carefully weigh these practical considerations with such benefits as mobility and flexibility. If you accept part-time or short-term employment from an institution or through a granting agency, consider checking the faculty or agency guidelines for institutional regulations, as well as state or local policies concerning your rights.

❖ 9 ❖

SURVIVING THE FIRST YEAR AS A
FACULTY MEMBER

THE MOST OBVIOUS THING ABOUT FIRST-YEAR TEACHING IS THE STAGGERING amount of time and effort required. You will get up early and stay up late preparing courses, day after day. Even if you think ahead for weeks between landing the job and entering the classroom, the plans will be incomplete and to a surprising extent unsuited to the class. Step back from your graduate student mentality in order to understand what brings undergraduates to the study of history. You should also prepare yourself psychologically to go from the top of the graduate hierarchy to the bottom of the faculty hierarchy. It's a step up but it's a step down too.

Most universities and colleges publish a faculty handbook that outlines what is expected academically and professionally at different stages. You should be given a handbook as soon as you arrive on campus. Do not hesitate to ask your chair, faculty dean or associate dean, or a personnel officer to clarify rules regarding all these issues. (The same applies to leaves, benefits, and so on.) Colleagues can be helpful but they may not be up-to-date, especially regarding tenure procedures and (changing) levels of expectations.

PREPARING FOR TEACHING

Many first-year teachers find it helpful to borrow more experienced colleagues' plans for courses as a means of getting started. This will spare you the long labor of contriving courses by yourself the first time through. You might also want to buy teaching packets, available from groups such as the Organization of American Historians. Course syllabi are also now published by different sources, such as Markus Wiener Publishers, and can be found online at H-Net and the AHA. Send away for lists of such materials as soon as you sign your employment contract and know what you will be teaching.

RESPONSIBILITIES OF A FACULTY MEMBER

Every college or university faculty has committee work, and you must expect to do your share. That means advising and serving on committees for your department and fulfilling other assignments, such as recruiting students or speaking to the public. This is all part of your job.

Expect to do your share of this sort of professional service to your university community, but do not let committee work drive you into the ground. New faculty especially will face plenty of pressures to join committees, so find out what an acceptable load is. Women and minorities are asked to do far more than their share of committee work in order to meet university equity criteria or diversify the lineup. Women are no longer rare creatures in most universities. But as long as female faculty in the university remain in a numerical minority, all those hard-fought-for, well-meaning gender equity policies will mean work for women. You do not want to be a casualty of this structural inequity.

DAILY LIFE IN THE DEPARTMENT

When you actually arrive in your department office, it is time to learn about the mores and services of office and department culture. You soon will enjoy some departmental services, such as secretarial help, but you may find that a hierarchy exists and, as a beginner, you come last. Learn how to make your requests as easy as possible on the staff and observe the practice of others. You quickly will understand the blessings and limits of clerical support and photocopying. Under no circumstances should you expect the office staff to handle private business. Remember, staff members are professionals and department colleagues.

You may also encounter a formal or informal division of acquisition money for the library. Be sure to use your share.

If you want office furniture or equipment, such as a computer or another chair, put in your request early. Money for such items tends to be scarce, and your department administrator will need a healthy list to make a strong claim for enlarging the department's share. It is best to ask about material things before you accept the job. Deans may have a large budget for initial costs, but once you've started the job without an allocation, it may be too late to request one.

Do not use department telephones for private calls or other university services for private business. Make long-distance calls or use express mail delivery only when these are authorized by department regulations.

GENERAL RULES OF THUMB

Learn what counts toward advancement in your position. Formal policies exist but need interpretation. Keep your eyes and ears open to learn what successful faculty members have done, but don't get too involved in trying to figure out what is appropriate behavior. You should speak when you have something to say, figure out when it's important to fight and when it is wiser to let things go, and work at building credibility as someone who is responsible. Do your departmental homework by reading files for personnel decisions, participating actively in searches, and completing general follow-up tasks, so that you have a chance of winning when it's time to fight.

In addition to an institutional handbook, some departments have a statement that covers most of the ground concerning conditions of employment. Study these guidelines—they will provide you with the foundation for getting along well with your colleagues.

POLICIES ON FAMILY LEAVE

All employees should be aware of the institution's policies concerning benefits and leaves. Lesbians and gay men, unmarried heterosexual couples, single parents—anyone involved in a domestic partnership, including marriage—should know if the institution's policies include leaves and if certain situations are covered by insurance policies, such as caring for an ill parent, partner, or child, or for maternity or parenting. Make no assumptions about your school's policies. Confirm school/insurance policies in writing with benefits personnel. If the school makes no provision for leaves, you may want to organize to change these policies.

TAKING ADVANTAGE OF LEAVE POLICIES

Having an academic job means that you can take leaves. If you know you and your partner will have to live apart, it becomes even more important to establish your department's policy on leaves and time off for extramural grants before you accept a position. You will have to weigh the advantages and disadvantages of letting your employer know your personal circumstances, but at the very least, you can determine what possibilities exist for time off.

Knowing when to ask about such possibilities can be tricky. You'll have to rely on your judgment and the advice of others who confront similar circumstances at your campus or in your department. If you find that your department is totally unsympathetic to your dilemma, then you should consider seeking another job more suited to your needs.

Take advantage of the enormous flexibility of academic schedules. No other job gives you as much as twenty to twenty-five weeks a year when you can work away from your office without employer supervision. No other job gives you such lengthy uninterrupted periods when you can leave your place of employment.

How to Maintain Your Privacy

The new faculty member may face a fairly busy social life. There are ritualistic events, such as a president's reception, a departmental cocktail party, or an all-campus picnic. Ask the chair about protocol whenever you are in doubt. There are still schools where the president's reception is formal. Beyond these obvious rites, you may be invited to parties by your colleagues. You should reciprocate once you are familiar with your colleagues' preferred forms of recreation. Sociability is necessary and enjoyable, in spite of the grueling routine of first-year teaching.

You may find it hard to maintain your privacy during your first year. As the newcomer, you will arouse curiosity. Expect questions from colleagues about your past, your future plans, and your personal life. Some may try to elicit your opinions about the department or school administration. Be careful—first-year stress may be getting to you, and unguarded answers may prove to be a problem later. Do not give in to a negative attitude. Deflect such questions by changing the subject. Handle awkward questions with as much professional aplomb as possible. Your novelty as a newcomer will soon wear off, and by term's end, first-year anxieties and demands will abate. Try to weather the storm without giving in to minor grievances. You will make acquaintances and friends worth keeping even among your most inquisitive colleagues. Try to make the best of the inevitably stressful first year.

Applying for Other Jobs

Once you are employed by an institution, don't feel obliged to stay simply because you feel fortunate to have a job. If you are unhappy with your job, department, or institution, consider a change. Some historians are finding it easier to move laterally within the profession. Consider lateral moves as a serious option at any time in your career. If you do seek another position, make it clear to your department that you are continuing to take seriously your obligations to them. You should place the emphasis on "opportunity" rather than "retreat."

❖ 10 ❖

TENURE AND PROMOTION

IN ALL LIKELIHOOD, YOUR UNIVERSITY'S POLICY IS THAT FACULTY MEMBERS MUST achieve success in the usual trio: teaching, research, and service. That sounds obvious, but learn what is specifically meant by that policy. At some schools, publishing a textbook or other teaching materials counts in the teaching column, in other schools it counts as research. Some institutions emphasize student enrollments, while others look for consistently favorable evaluations by students and faculty. Learn what aspect of teaching is important. Find out if the school expects you to bring in research grants.

Almost immediately, you should get into the habit of keeping records and building up a personnel file. Keep class grade lists, course outlines, notes, and evaluations, if available. Keep copies of anything written for institutional business, publication, or public presentation, as well as reviews of your work. Inform your chair of all your accomplishments. Many departments will have faculty activity sheets. Again, be sure to record all your accomplishments: publications, student supervision, guest-speaking engagements, works-in-progress, research grants, and prizes or other academic honors. In short, never allow yourself to suffer an incomplete departmental evaluation because you are not well organized. Conditions for promotion were set before you got the job. Don't judge your performance by the standards set by some tenured faculty. You need to accept that there is a divergence of expectations, and that you may be asked to accomplish more than the people judging you.

Service can be an external and vague category. Some schools will accept anything, from service speeches at Rotary Clubs to attendance at professional meetings. Elsewhere, you may find service defined primarily as being for the wider professional community, with everything else given minor attention. Others define service as an exact portion of your time devoted to departmental and collegiate administration. Once you understand the categories, you can figure out how to do your best to satisfy the institution's requirements.

TENURE

In academic life—and in some related professional employments—one of the best-known goals is achieving tenure status. If you do not get tenure, the institution is unlikely to retain your services. If you do, you have security in your job against nearly everything except your own gross dereliction of duty, attrition through change in academic policy, retrenchment, bankruptcy of the school, action of a legislature, or natural disaster.

Tenure in the university is meant to protect academic freedom and integrity, but it also provides professors with a degree of job security that few other members of our society enjoy.

Tenure is a special relationship between one faculty member and one institution, with benefits to be enjoyed by both parties. The practice of conferring tenure has become so nearly standard throughout American academia as to be regarded as a right by many people. It is no such thing. Most people receive tenure if, and only if, they have satisfied the particular requirements of their institution. To be sure, in some institutions, faculty unions have made conditions for achieving tenure part of a collective rather than individual agreement, which makes promotion to tenure seem rather routine.

The requirements for attaining tenure and the procedure for conferring it vary only slightly. Generally, there are time limits. The American Association of University Professors (AAUP) has tried to standardize a probationary period of no more than six years for those hired initially with the PhD and no more than seven years for those hired without it. The tenure decision should be reached during the academic year preceding the last one in the probationary period, so someone passed over may have adequate time to search for another job. Most schools observe something close to this formula, but quite a few stretch the probationary period in one way or another, usually in cases of exceptional scholarship and previous teaching experience.

TENURE PROCEDURE

Normally the tenure procedure begins with a recommendation from the members of your department who already have tenure. If your department favors your candidacy, their decision goes to the dean, sometimes through a committee composed of faculty from a variety of disciplines. The idea is to achieve some ineffable uniformity of standards or to put a check on the arbitrary will of the dean. If the dean agrees, the recommendation is put before the higher administrators and the institution's governing board, where review is often perfunctory. If the decision at the department level is against you, insist on an explanation, and in that light, perhaps a reconsideration. If the decision is in your favor, the dean may reject it and give reasons. You can appeal an adverse ruling and should learn your institution's procedures for doing so. If you have good reason to fear a negative decision on the basis of gender or racial prejudice, you will want to consult your institution's anti-discrimination policies beforehand. (Also see "Dealing with Discrimination" below, and Chapter 11, "Grievances," for related information.)

Make sure you are clear about the tenure procedures of your department and college. Seek advice from the relevant support staff in academic personnel or the dean's and president's offices. Your chair may not be aware of all details, and even if you have department backing, the chair may not be able to give you complete information.

Some schools have begun a pre-tenure evaluation that can be frightening but helpful. In this arrangement, you are looked over in your third or fourth year, or sometimes yearly. Colleagues observe you in the classroom, read your work, and offer a written summary of their thoughts on your progress. This evaluation can let you know how well you are proceeding.

You will be painfully aware of what is going on in your tenure review. Today, in an era of litigiousness and fervor for due process, reviews are more formalized and drawn out. You will discuss your case with senior colleagues. They may visit your classes, often with elaborate pre-arrangements that are likely to provoke anxiety. You will take part in preparing your case by going over your record, rounding up copies of your publications, and distributing students' evaluations. You are told the gist of what was said during the actual tenure conference, ostensibly for self-improvement. You may even be in a position to bargain. That is, if you have not met all the requirements, you may be granted a postponement of the final decision.

DEALING WITH DISCRIMINATION

If you believe you were denied tenure or due process due to discrimination, be prepared to show that others got tenure on the basis of similar records. This will allow you to draw comparisons of achievement or to provide well-substantiated allegations of discrimination on the basis of sex, racial, or ethnic background. Regardless of how you frame your case, you will have to gather a great deal of evidence and present it convincingly. Whatever the rules say, the burden of proof is on you, so you may find it helpful to hire a lawyer. You should also ask yourself whether you want to remain with colleagues who have treated you unfairly. Even if you don't, however, the vindication of your professional success may well be worth a fight.

It is far better and far easier to prevent than to undo discrimination against you on non-professional grounds. Prejudice against female scholars runs much deeper than it appears, especially if they are feminists, mothers, lesbians, minority women, or commuters. Their writings are often underestimated. As Darlene Clark Hine stated in the summary of the 1986 American Studies Association report, "Personal Lives and Professional Careers: The Uneasy Balance":

Black women professors must tackle head-on the problems of having their research and scholarship taken seriously. Women, for the most part, remain recent and still-powerless immigrants in the academy. They still have to work twice as hard and be three times better just to be perceived as average and win tenure and promotion.

No matter what reasons you have for expecting discriminatory treatment in the review for tenure, ask advice from faculty women's/African American/gay and lesbian/Hispanic or other campus caucuses. Visit the school's affirmative action officer if you think that will help, although sometimes the officer's main concern will be in keeping the university out of lawsuits. The officer can assemble the data to show presumption of a pattern of discrimination or can get the administrators to pay for unusual procedures, such as review of the tenure deliberations by impartial outsiders. Maybe this officer, by monitoring your department, can inspire more scrupulous behavior than would otherwise occur.

If you want to challenge your department's recommendation or the reversal of a favorable recommendation higher up the administrative ladder, consult your local chapter of the American Association of University Professors immediately. If there is not a local chapter, contact the AAUP's national headquarters or the American Historical Association.

PROMOTION

Most institutions rank faculty as assistant, associate, and full professors. Promotion brings a higher salary, more prestige inside and outside of the institution, and often new responsibilities. As an associate or full professor you will be asked to serve on more committees in and out of the institution, and you will be called upon to evaluate for promotion peers in other institutions. Junior faculty will be more likely to regard you as a mentor and to ask for guidance and advice on their professional lives.

If you are a new full-time faculty member with a completed degree, you are usually hired as an assistant professor. You can expect to remain in that position until you are granted tenure and promoted to associate professor. In unusual circumstances, you may be promoted to associate professor before you become eligible for tenure. In most cases, early promotion virtually ensures tenure later on. Sometimes, tenure is awarded without promotion when the faculty member fails to fulfill to the letter the promotion requirements, but the department or institution is willing to grant tenure nonetheless. It bears repeating, however, that such cases are unusual.

Requirements for promotion vary not only at major research universities, but at smaller colleges as well. A record of publication, however, is increasingly an essential element, not only in large universities, but in colleges as well. It is wise to determine your institution's policies as soon as possible. The first few years are difficult; you are busy writing lectures and preparing classes and have little time to pursue research and writing, except in the summer. Beyond the first few years, you should work toward meeting your institution's requirements, and set aside time during the academic year to attend to your own scholarly work.

It is almost as important to attend conferences in your field as it is to publish. It will increase your visibility and help you to develop contacts within your field. Often when you come up for promotion and/or tenure, you are asked to provide a list of individuals who are competent to evaluate your scholarship and overall merit. It is helpful to know about a half dozen people who share your interests and who are sympathetic to your approach. Attending conferences is a good way to get to know people professionally and to keep up with scholarship. It also provides the sort of intellectual exchange that can be difficult to find in institutions where no one shares your particular interests.

Tenure and promotion to associate professor usually occur simultaneously. Although departments generally specify the time you must spend as an assistant professor before you are promoted, there is no such clear-cut time frame for promotion from associate to full professor. Some people remain associate professors for their entire career; others get promoted within a few years. Usually promotion to full professor requires significant achievement in the years since promotion to the associate level. Time in the ranks alone is rarely sufficient. Here, too, you should try to get a clear sense of what is required to meet the criteria.

Promotion from associate to full professor seems to occur more slowly for women than for men. Some of this is due to sexism, to the unwillingness of colleagues to recognize women's scholarly merit, and to the undervaluation of women's work in the academy as elsewhere. If you feel you legitimately deserve promotion and are being denied it on sexist grounds, do something about it.

❖ 11 ❖

GRIEVANCES

MOST COLLEGES AND UNIVERSITIES HAVE DEVELOPED QUASI-JUDICIAL procedures for hearing grievances. Under the best circumstances, procedures are written and all members of faculty and staff receive copies of the rules. In other cases, less is committed to paper and the institution does little to make the procedures known. If this is the case at your institution, you might want to consider organizing to formalize grievance procedures. All levels of faculty and students deserve legitimate and fair recourse for grievances.

In all probability, most grievances will be internal and will raise questions that belong in the department. Many complaints can be addressed in a conference with your department chair or supervisor. The supervisor's job is to facilitate the faculty's professional endeavors. A conscientious chair should take your word for what will benefit the department and will look for ways to settle any conflicts.

Conflicts may occur between you and your supervisor, however, and usually a short discussion with the person next up the ladder, such as a dean, will suffice. Maybe you will think better of the case and withdraw the complaint. Maybe your dean will speak to your immediate supervisor. When going through these channels, resist any urges you have to talk generally on your feelings about the institution. Stick to the immediate issues, and always state your problem in professional terms. Any indication of personal gripes is likely to be received with impatience or dismissed.

Faculty committees may be part of the grievance procedure. They may evaluate applications for research grants or special awards for launching new courses, advise the dean on promotions or tenure, and guard against rejecting deserved promotions and raises. If you think you have been wronged by one of these committees, it may be difficult to bring a complaint. The committees are intended to make decisions on the basis of collective evaluations rather than individual judgments, so the members are obliged to say little about their deliberations. Your best bet is to consult the relevant dean or to discreetly ask friends who know members of the committee. You must know precisely what your complaint is about and how to express it and prove it, if you are to make a successful claim. If these methods fail, look around to find a plausible next step for your appeal. You may also have to consider the possibility that your hopes have been unreasonable.

The most likely trouble spot is an abusive administration where the grievance procedures are likely to be absent or rudimentary. If grievance procedures exist, the administrators may try to keep them out of sight. In other cases, department chairs have been known to deny a faculty member's request for access to the university's operations manual or budget. In the face of such conduct, you may feel helpless. Help may be available from the dean or may require outside consultation. Your first task is to find a way to initiate action to protect yourself. First ask your chair, then the dean or other colleagues, about applicable rules— where you can read them and which appeals are open to you. It is important to verify procedures in writing whenever possible.

If your institution offers a quasi-judicial grievance hearing, use it when the situation requires it. Speak to the school's affirmative action officer or, if necessary, consider consulting a lawyer. There is a growing body of law and precedent on these hearings, which a good attorney will be able to explain.

Where local channels are blocked or do not exist, write to the American Association of University Professors' national headquarters and to the American Historical Association. The AAUP will look into your complaint and will make a concerted effort to determine and redress wrongs without embarrassing the complainant (plaintiff). The AHA's Professional Division looks into grievances brought to its attention but follows strict policy rules pertaining to such procedures. The AHA also generally has a policy of staying out of such disputes until procedures on the complainant's local level have been pursued to little or no avail.

❖ 12 ❖

HOW TO GET ON A PROGRAM AT A PROFESSIONAL MEETING

THE ROLE OF THE PROGRAM COMMITTEE

Program committees are required to develop a program that is balanced geographically, chronologically, and topically. To do so, they generally welcome proposals from a variety of potential participants. Some program committees prefer to select commentators themselves; others gladly take suggestions. More detailed information about programs can often be found in the newsletters of different associations. The following will hardly guarantee your participation but should increase your chances by describing some of the elements a program committee will look for.

GETTING ONTO A PROGRAM

SUBJECT

Rules vary for submitting paper proposals. Some organizations require a complete panel. Others accept single papers. In most cases you should try to submit a complete panel rather than a single paper. Individual papers should clearly relate and should focus on historically significant problems.

PARTICIPANTS

In choosing participants, your first aim should be a strong panel. You should make every effort to find scholars who have not been program participants in the past year. Balance the panel with regard to gender, minorities, rank, regions, and type of institution. If papers are to be given by younger members of the profession, it is often desirable that at least one of the commentators be a person of established reputation.

SUBMITTING THE PANEL

Have one person coordinate all of the papers and write up the proposal so that a unified panel is submitted. Briefly explain in the cover letter the purpose and significance of the panel and its appropriate historical categories. For example, one panel might cover American history, family history, and urban history. Include relevant background information on participants. Explain their expertise in the subjects under discussion. Be concise and to the point.

Enclose a description of the panel as it would appear in the program. This includes titles for the session and the papers. Consult an old program for form and study the guidelines in calls for papers. Provide a brief statement about the panel's purpose and importance with a short summary of each paper's thesis or program. Keep the entire statement short and succinct.

SUBMIT THE PROPOSAL EARLY

Submit the proposal well in advance of the deadlines. Send the proposal and cover letter to the program committee chair. The chair keeps a log of all panels and proposals submitted and sends copies for appraisal to the members of the committee who are particularly concerned with each field. The member who reviews your proposal may write to you about it, asking you to clarify questions. It is your responsibility to check journals, newsletters, and so forth for information on deadlines as well as program committee membership. Some programs are prepared almost two years in advance, so don't allow the deadline to slip by.

If the proposal is turned down and you are convinced it is a sound plan, consider offering it again the following year. Your topics may have been treated by a surfeit of other proposals for that particular meeting. In any event, be prepared to wait several months after the committee's deadline for final notification of acceptance or rejection. In the meantime, however, you may receive word of tentative approval from the chair or an encouraging hint from the member who evaluated your proposal.

PRESENTING THE PAPER

Once you have agreed to participate in a session, make every effort to fulfill that agreement. If you are to present a paper, allow ample time to write the very best one you can. In most cases, you will be told exactly how long your presentation should be, so plan accordingly. You can count on reading a page in about two minutes, so keep your paper short enough to stay within the time assigned. The person who chairs the session has the duty to cut off presentations after the allotted time has expired. You don't want to be asked to sit down just before you have reached that eloquent climax. Also, make sure you submit a copy of your paper to the panel's commentators, about one month ahead of time.

As you prepare your paper, remember that several people, perhaps prospective employers, may request a copy. While the organization and style of the text will be designed for a listening audience, use footnotes to gear your paper to a reading audience as well.

Always give your paper an advance performance, if possible before a large audience. Women might think of a women's caucus within their department, but if your department has a colloquium that draws a larger crowd and you feel comfortable with the paper and the audience, take advantage of this opportunity to rehearse. Junior faculty may find that this experience can become an ersatz mid-career review, a second job talk, or a pre-tenure review, and choose not to engage in this anxiety-producing effort. Nevertheless, the best criticism often comes from colleagues whose fields and perspectives differ from your own.

One of the major goals in presenting a paper may be to build your c.v. But remember that the more important goal is to share your ideas and receive responses to them from the audience. Go into your session prepared for this intellectual give-and-take.

❖ 13 ❖

GETTING PUBLISHED

HISTORIANS COMMUNICATE SCHOLARSHIP ORALLY, VISUALLY, AND IN WRITING. They teach and speak; they create and consult on media projects, exhibits, or other cultural resources; and they publish. For scholars, publishing is perhaps the most important way to communicate the results of scholarship. Publishing is one of the responsibilities as well as one of the joys of being a historian, and most historians enjoy both research and writing.

As a historian, you will want to present your scholarship in a variety of media to reach the broadest possible audience, but you will also want to communicate to colleagues in a more specialized language. Learn how to present your work in different styles for different audiences, but make sure that it is always based on careful research and, written in excellent prose, with a broad intellectual scope. Never publish anything but the best work you are capable of.

Academic historians are expected by colleagues and school administrations to document their scholarly activities in a particular way during their initial untenured years. It is best to learn about this process in graduate school, from peers and publishers. Promotion often rests with the perception of your publication record, so you must be conscious of how your colleagues judge publishing. If you know what criteria they use, you will be able to present your work in the most effective way. Public historians must balance the requirements of their varied activities and publication in public history against writing and research that focus more narrowly on traditional history.

How much publishing is enough? Standards vary by department. Seek out and familiarize yourself with departmental guidelines regarding publication for promotion and tenure. These policies should be clearly stated by your employer and must guide your publication strategy.

Turning Your Thesis into a Book

Most dissertations need to be revised with two things in mind: trimming detail and eliminating a defensive tone in favor of confident statements and carefully selected illustrations. Most authors need to rewrite rather than do further research. You are being asked to shift from the vantage point of a graduate student proving yourself worthy of attention, to an "expert" who can discuss the relevant historiography with broad strokes (rather than a blow-by-blow account of the literature) and reach bold generalizations without sacrificing the specificity and richness of the case study or subject at hand. This will take some time and effort, and should be done before officially submitting a manuscript to a publisher.

Finding a Publisher for a Monograph or Book

Normally, the scholarly monograph is viewed by the profession as the most significant work to publish for promotion and tenure. For tenure review, some departments will be content just to see your manuscript; others will insist on seeing a contract or even a published book.

These differing demands may dictate your publishing strategy. Never publish a book that you do not consider an important contribution to the literature of your field, but do not expect your first book to be a "great book." Make it as good as you can, send it into the world, and look forward to your next effort. Be aware that different publishers have different timetables and different reputations for efficiency and treatment of authors. Do not be afraid to call several scholars who have published with a press to find out how they were treated. Scholars publishing their second or third books and who think their topic appeals to a wider audience may want to discuss their work with a literary agent.

You may send a query and a proposal to more than one editor, but once a press asks to read your manuscript, do not submit it to anyone else for consideration until you know whether or not that publisher wants to publish your work.

In your proposal, you should:

1. Submit a brief description of the scope of the book, the sources used, methodologies employed, and its significance to the literature in the field.

2. Suggest a potential market. Would it be useful in courses in paperback? Who would read it and why?

3. Indicate the length of the manuscript, sections that are incomplete, need revision, or require scholarly updates. If the manuscript is or was a dissertation, state your plans for revision, as a dissertation will need editing and revision before it can be published as a book.

4. Include information on the form of the manuscript. If your book has been written on a word processor, indicate the kind of software used. Some publishers may not use authors' diskettes, so keep the format and files simple. Do not use elaborate codes to indicate chapter, subheads, or chart heads with bold or italic type or symbols, since these will be reformatted to fit the publisher's design and typesetting equipment. If the publisher requests a copy of the manuscript, submit two clean, easy-to-read copies. Charts or illustrations may be submitted on separate sheets. Any marks on the manuscript should be made clearly and in pencil.

5. Enclose a copy of your c.v.

Your cover letter *may* mention persons in the field who are competent to judge the manuscript. The editor, however, is not obliged to follow your suggestions. It is wise to exclude friends and mentors to avoid the possibility of favoritism or bias.

To find a publisher for your work, study ads, publishers' lists, and the *Literary Market Place* or the *Writer's Market*. Look at your own bookshelves—that usually provides a good preliminary survey of which presses are doing the best or the most publishing in your particular field. Another good source of information is *Getting Published: The Acquisition Process at University Presses*, published by the University of Tennessee Press. Be aware of vanity presses. Publishing with one will most likely not help your tenure concerns if this is your first book.

Editors will usually read your manuscript, pay an honorarium to outside readers for an evaluation, and prepare reports for their publications board on the commercial viability of publishing your work. If your manuscript is ultimately rejected by a publisher who was seriously considering it, you are then free to submit it to another press. If the publisher suggests revisions that you are not prepared to make, you may cut off negotiations and begin the process with another publisher.

Once you have been notified of an editor's interest in your manuscript, you will doubtless have questions about the publishing process. Many questions cannot be addressed until the manuscript is accepted and a contract offered, but here are some questions to keep in mind when you enter into serious discussions with the publisher:

- How long will it take to find out if the manuscript is accepted for publication?
- How long will it take for contract negotiations?
- How long will production take?
- Who pays the cost of illustrations?
- What are the publisher's plans for marketing?
- How many copies will be printed?

- Will hardcover and paperback editions be published?
- Will the paperback be published simultaneously?
- If not, how long before the paperback is released?
- What, if any, are the royalty agreements/advances?

If you have any doubts about the answers you receive, be sure to speak to other authors to get a different perspective. Do not act hastily. Consider all factors: editing, marketing, rights and royalties, contract negotiations, and publisher's reputation before deciding on one publisher over another. Once a publisher has expressed a clear interest in your book, it is not appropriate to initiate negotiations with other publishers.

DEALING WITH REJECTIONS

All authors accumulate rejection letters. You will, too. If the scholarship and interpretations you present are sound, you will eventually find a publisher. Determine if the rejection was due to a general publishing decision—marketing or the product. Sometimes budgetary or other considerations may be the cause of the rejection. If you are unsure about your writing style, study historians whose style you admire or sign up for a technical writing workshop at your university. These courses are often very helpful for learning good expository writing techniques and for developing organizing strategies. Ask colleagues, other scholars, or mentors to review the work.

A rejection may simply mean that you have not found the right publisher. Seek advice from colleagues whose work you respect. Continue to look for editors who are likely to be interested in your subject. Query letters may bring ten to twenty rejections for every one or two invitations to read the manuscript. Normally you will want to try two or three presses before beginning major revisions or resubmission. If the problem seems to be scholarship, interpretation, or style (or all three) you must be prepared to re-evaluate and revise your manuscript.

PUBLICATION PROCEDURES

It will take about a year from the time you submit the manuscript until you see a finished book. Usually the copyeditor's revisions and final page proofs can be managed along with your other professional responsibilities, but once the contract is signed and the book goes into production, your job may be far from over. Depending on the publisher's schedule and budget, you may be asked to approve editing; proofread and correct the typeset pages; compile the index; provide clean, easily reproduced charts, tables, maps, or illustrations—all in a relatively short period of time. Personal and professional demands may compete with publication deadlines. Whenever possible, it would be to your advantage to try to schedule large projects, such as indexing, during school breaks. This is not always possible because of publishing schedules, but it is worth inquiring about. A possible alternative would be to hire an indexer. However, this often costs several hundred dollars, and you may be required to pay for such freelance services. There are indexing software packages available, and this may be a good solution. Such concerns should be addressed during contract negotiations.

A copyeditor will pore over your final manuscript for grammar, organization, and style, and make many suggestions for editing revisions (for example, to eliminate concluding paragraphs that are really introductions to the next chapter). You will have about a month to review and approve these changes. You may be surprised at the amount of copyediting done. Generally, a copyeditor actually helps your prose. Be tough-skinned. Often the changes are not corrections to "bad" grammar but are made to conform to the press' style sheet (e.g., changing World War II to the Second World War).

Read the changes carefully. It is okay to disagree with the copyeditor. For example, in breaking down a run-on sentence, the copyeditor may have changed the intended meaning of the original sentence. Finally, you proofread the typeset pages, at which point you are to make only absolutely necessary changes.

PROBLEMS WITHIN A PUBLISHING HOUSE

Stability is important in any business relationship, particularly when dealing with a publisher and editor. If a publisher sells out or merges, you may be faced with a suspended publishing program. A publisher may try to cancel or buy out your contract, or publish but not market your book. Transitions at small or large commercial publishers can be difficult to weather. University presses tend to be more stable, but editors still move around. Adjustment to changes in staff at your publisher can also be trying and problematic. Your editor may move to another press and want to take you along, if you have not already signed a contract. A new editor may be a novice, in a different field, have different interests, or not be able to recognize your contribution as quickly as another. Sound out the new editor. Ask questions. Make your interests known.

PUBLISHING ARTICLES IN SCHOLARLY JOURNALS

Make sure you know which journals the profession as a whole and your colleagues in particular consider the most scholarly and prestigious. If you are in a field about which your colleagues know little, you should explain in a memo to the department why this journal is important in the field. If you publish in journals not well known to historians, try to achieve a balance by submitting articles to journals that are better known in the profession. Should you be unable to do so, there may be consequences in terms of recognition and evaluation of your work by colleagues and administration. While it is important to reach the widest possible audience with your writing, in the early years of your career it is necessary to balance this goal carefully against the reality that the department and university within which you are seeking tenure will almost always be the final arbiter. Publishing a scholarly article in a professional journal can be gratifying and good for your resume. Even if your article is not immediately accepted, the publishing process can be rewarding, since you will probably receive evaluations of your work from experts in your field.

You may already have in mind a journal where you would like to publish your article. If not, review journals in your field with an eye toward matching your article with a journal likely to publish it. You might consider, for example, the length of articles a journal tends to publish, its orientation in the discipline, the composition of the editorial board, and the tone of its articles. One important consideration is whether the journal uses a "peer-review" process in which manuscripts are evaluated by several academic experts, rather than by the editor alone. Peer-reviewed journals are held in highest esteem in the profession. Faculty and advanced graduate students can offer important insights and advice about journals' practices and may help steer your decision. A journal's copyright page should provide guidelines for submission of manuscripts to that journal, i.e., whether it reviews unsolicited manuscripts, preferred style, number of copies to send, the address, etc.

Generally, journals do not review articles that are simultaneously under consideration elsewhere or that contain already-published material. Once you have selected a journal, you should consider revising your article to fit what seem to be that journal's standards or tone. Mail in your article, following the protocols outlined on the copyright page. You may include a cover page indicating your contact information and that you wish to have the manuscript considered for publication. Wait. You should receive acknowledgment that your manuscript was received, but after that, you are at the mercy of the journal's editorial process, which is often quite lengthy. In a peer-reviewed journal, your article will be sent to readers, the readers will write reports, the editor will compile the reports, and then she will make a decision about your article. All of this may take months. You will receive one of three basic responses from the journal: your article is accepted; you are asked to revise it and resubmit it, with no guarantee that it will be accepted later; or your article is rejected. In many cases, the editor will send you the readers' reports, which can aid in your revision process, even if this particular journal has rejected your article. If your article is accepted, you continue your relationship with this journal as the article is edited for publication. If not, do not be discouraged! Re-evaluate your work in light of the reviews you received. Then choose another journal and send it out again.

Resist the tendency to cannibalize your book by publishing chapters. If possible, maintain the integrity of your work by publishing it whole, while the material is fresh, so you do not jeopardize your chance to reach the best possible audience. Publishing one article is a good idea because it establishes you as an authority on the subject, alerts others in your field to your larger work, brings criticism from scholars that you can incorporate into the final version of your book, and may attract the attention of a potential editor. Many journals have backlogs, so remember that publication of an article may take longer than publication of the book. Also be aware that book publishers often prefer to be the first to publish your work, so before submitting an article or chapter from your book to a journal, it may be wise to negotiate this first with your publisher.

If you have research that was collected during your project but will not be included in the book, by all means submit it separately to a journal. In the explanatory note indicate how it relates to your larger work. If an article is based on your dissertation, list the dissertation title in a footnote. However, do not mention a title for an as-yet-unpublished book. Titles often change in the publishing process, and if you publish an incorrect title, it will haunt you for years as your future colleagues or students attempt to locate your book and cannot find it.

BOOK REVIEWS

Writing book reviews is a part of your life as a scholar. To receive book review work, register with the *Journal of American History* and the *American Historical Review* and specialized journals such as the *Journal of the Early Republic*, *Social Science History*, or *Journal of Women's History*. Most journals have forms that you are asked to fill out to let the editor know your special fields of expertise. You may also ask to review an individual book if you have special knowledge in the field or something important to say about a particular work. Do not ask or consent to review books written by friends or mentors. Professional acquaintance, however, is no reason to reject an invitation to review a book unless you feel somehow unable to provide a careful, objective analysis of the book, or you feel somehow that if you reviewed an acquaintance's book, it would unduly promote or sabotage the work.

Given your time constraints, do not review too many books. You might consider applying the "rule of two." Two a year is plenty unless you are asked to review an important book for an important journal. How do you decide which review work to accept and which to refuse? As mentioned earlier, ask colleagues which journals they read and respect. This has the added advantage of indicating how they will consider your reviews. If opinions differ widely about which journals to submit book reviews to, seek opinions from a broader range of your colleagues, and try to get a consensus. Book reviewers should respect their colleagues and review the book on its scholarly merits. This is not an opportunity for the reviewer to describe the book that he or she would have written.

Finding the time to write and sign on with a publisher for your monographs is a challenge to any beginning historian. As you progress in the profession, you may find that your schedule will permit more time to devote to publishing. There is a great deal of information on publishing available if you know where to look. Make a point of keeping up with publishers' catalogs and the book review sections of major journals, even if you only have time to skim through them.

❖ CONCLUSION ❖

BECOMING A HISTORIAN WAS MEANT TO GIVE THE NOVICE HISTORIAN A NECESSARILY brief glimpse into a vast and varied field. This overview was intended to advise and interest students in a profession that by definition continually redefines itself. A chief aim of this manual has been to promote the many benefits and positive aspects of the historical profession: the reward of service, the scholarly achievement, and the intellectual stimulation of steady growth and learning. Sadly, concerns about better opportunities for women, people of color, and gays and lesbians have yet to be specifically addressed in many areas of the profession. So another necessary aim has been to alert, inform, and empower students when they are faced with some of the inequities within the profession.

The historical profession can offer women and men a variety of careers and chances to broaden and refine intellectual interests. Although academia is the largest area of employment, positions in public history, archives, and other specialized fields have grown in recent years. It is the author's and contributors' hope that *Becoming a Historian* offers ideas to beginning historians, and the incentive to take advantage of—and eventually contribute to—the wealth of resources available. The "how-tos" of choosing a field of study, writing effective applications, finding funding, dealing with the tension of job searches, interviewing, and surviving in the profession have hopefully provided you with practical, applicable advice. Forethought, skill, and diligence will accomplish the rest.

❖ APPENDIX A ❖

A CHECKLIST OF JOB INTERVIEW QUERIES

THE FOLLOWING IS A CHECKLIST OF QUESTIONS AND CONCERNS TO BEAR IN MIND during the interview process. The information is addressed to historians in an academic environment, but the details pertain to public historians' concerns as well. It may help you make a more informed decision as you consider a major professional or geographic move.

ACADEMIC CONCERNS

TEACHING AND PEDAGOGY

- subjects
- undergraduate/graduate courses
- class size/average academic ability of students
- course development opportunities
- examination policies
- textbook policies: required/optional
- teaching/research assistants
- equipment resources: media, maps, networks
- student/graduate thesis advising
- committee membership responsibilities

ADMINISTRATIVE CONCERNS

OFFICE
- size/location
- equipment: computer software/hardware, bookshelves, filing cabinets, phone

DEPARTMENT/INSTITUTIONAL SUPPORT SERVICES
- secretarial/clerical help
- manuscript preparation
- word-processing capabilities
- computer services
- statistical/data analysis software availability
- photocopying services
- graphics/printing capabilities
- telephone/fax/telecommunications/mail facilities/policies

GOVERNANCE SYSTEMS
- department/faculty/institutional/campus
- union representation

CAMPUS SECURITY
- parking/other transportation
- security personnel
- distribution of keys/passes
- grounds lighting
- campus emergency services: phones/fire/police/medical facilities

LIBRARY RESOURCES
- monograph/serial holdings
- reserve policies
- audiovisual material/microfilm/microfiche
- purchasing policies/interlibrary loan services
- support staff
- faculty carrels

BENEFITS
- promotion/tenure policies
- salary: review/raise policies
- retirement programs: TIAA/CREF or other programs
- credit union within institution
- health insurance: dental, optical, full medical, disability
- family/paternal/maternal leave
- child care provision
- leave/sabbatical policies

Research and Professional Development

Faculty Teaching Development and Support
- departmental/college faculty seminars
- local funding programs
- support for regional/national grant proposals
- campus grants officer

Research Support
- conferences/research: grants or leaves/seminars/workshops

Community Environment

Cost of Living
- housing: availability and cost
- local/state tax structure
- insurance: home/car
- food/services/entertainment

Community Resources
- public safety services: fire/police/ambulance, road maintenance
- parking and public transportation
- recycling programs
- community groups
- shopping/banking
- local medical services
- daycare facilities/public and private schools
- libraries
- religious services

Entertainment and Recreation
- indoor/outdoor activities
- restaurants
- community clubs/organizations
- theaters: movie/local stage company
- sports
- nightlife
- arts community

Local Government
- local/county/city/state legislative

❖ Appendix B ❖

Selected Professional Organizations
and Publications

LISTED BELOW ARE ORGANIZATIONS THAT GRADUATE STUDENTS AND NOVICE historians will find relevant to their pursuit of information about the historical profession. Much of the text is derived from *Careers for Students of History* by Barbara J. Howe, published by the American Historical Association and the National Council on Public History. This is by no means a complete list nor is it a recommendation. The *Directory of Affiliated Societies*, available on the AHA web site at http://www.theaha.org/affiliates/, is also a good resource. The annual *Encyclopedia of Associations* provides information on thousands of organizations. It should be available, along with other comprehensive resources, at major public and school libraries.

If no publication date is given, the publication cited is a periodical or annual directory.

ACT, Inc., P.O. Box 168, 2201 N. Dodge St., Iowa City, IA 52243-0168. (319) 337-1000. Web page: http://www.act.org.

Advisory Council on Historic Preservation, 1100 Pennsylvania Ave., NW, Ste. 809, Washington, DC 20004. (202) 606-8503/8505. Fax (202) 606-8647/8672. E-mail: achp@achp.gov. Web page: http://www.achp.gov.

Affirmative Action Register, 8356 Olive Blvd., St. Louis, MO 63132. (314) 991-1335/(800) 537-0655. Fax (314) 997-1788. E-mail: aareeo@ concentric.net. Web page: http://www.aar-eeo.com.

American Association for State and Local History, 1717 Church St., Nashville, TN 37203-2991. (615) 320-3203. Fax (615) 327-9013. E-mail: history@aaslh.org. Web page: http://www.aaslh.org.

Publications: *History News; History News Dispatch* (www. aaslh.org/dispatchonline.htm); *Directory of Historical Organizations in the United States and Canada*, 15th ed. (2001); Carol Kammen and Norma Prendergast, eds., *Encyclopedia of Local History* (2000); Carol Kammen, *On Doing Local History:*

Reflections on What Local Historians Do, Why, and What It Means (1996); extensive list of books, audiovisual materials, and technical leaflets

American Association of Community Colleges, National Center for Higher Education, 1 Dupont Circle, NW, Ste. 410, Washington, DC 20036. (202) 728-0200. Fax (202) 833-2467. Web page: http://www.aacc.nche.edu.

Publications: *AACC Letter; Community College Times, Community College Journal*

American Association of Museums, 1575 Eye St., NW, Ste. 400, Washington, DC 20005. (202) 289-1818. Fax (202) 289-6578. Web page: http://www.aam-us.org.

Job listings: Aviso (http://www.aviso.aam-us.org/)

Publications: *Museum News; The Official Museum Directory* (2000); *1999 AAM Museum Financial Information Survey* (2000); *Careers in Museums: A Variety of Vocations* (1994); Jane R. Glaser and Artemis A. Zenetou, *Museums: A Place to Work—Planning Museum Careers* (1996); G. Ellis Burcaw, *Introduction to Museum Work* (1997)

American Association of University Professors, 1012 14th St., NW, Ste. 500, Washington, DC 20005-3465. (202) 737-5900. Fax (202) 737-5526. E-mail: aaup@aaup.org. Web page: http://www.aaup.org.

Publications: *Academe* (http://www.aaup.org/publications/Academe/index .htm); *Collective Bargaining Congress News* (http://www.aaup.org/Faculty-Org/cbc/Cbnews.htm)

American Bar Association, 750 N. Lake Shore Dr., Chicago, IL 60611. Web page: http://www.abanet.org.

American Historical Association, 400 A St., SE, Washington, DC 20003. (202) 544-2422. Fax (202) 544-8307. Web page: http://www.theaha.org.

Job listings: *Perspectives* (online at http://www.theaha.org /members/eibs/search_form.cfm)

Publications: *American Historical Review*; *Perspectives* (http://www.theaha. org/perspectives); *Directory of History Departments, Historical Organizations, and Historians; Careers for Students of History,* by Constance Schulz, Page Putnam Miller, Aaron Marrs, and Kevin Allen, with the National Council on Public History, and the Public History Program, University of South Carolina; *We Shall Gladly Teach,* by Terry B. Seip

Online publications on the profession: http://www.theaha.org/ pubs/olpubs.htm (includes "Liberal Learning and the History Major" and *Statement on Standards of Professional Conduct*)

American Library Association, 50 E. Huron, Chicago, IL 60611. (800) 545-2433. TDD (312) 944-7298. Fax (312) 440-9374. Web page: http://www.ala.org.

American Studies Association, 1120 19th St., NW, Ste. 301, Washington, DC 20036. (202) 467-4783. Fax (202) 467-4786. E-mail: asastaff@erols.com. Web page: http://www.georgetown.edu/crossroads/asainfo.html.

Association for Documentary Editing. Web page: http://etext.lib. virginia.edu/ade/ (includes online listings for employment working with documentary collections).

Association for Living History, Farm, and Agricultural Museums, Judith Sheridan, Secretary/Treasurer, 8774 Rte. 45 NW, North Bloomfield, OH 44450. Fax (216) 685-4410. E-mail: sheridan@orwell.net. Web page: http://www.alhfam.org.

Association of American Publishers, 50 F St., NW, Washington, DC 20001-1564. (202) 347-3375. Fax (202) 347-3690. Web page: http://www. publishers.org.
Publications: *AAP Monthly Report*; *Newsletter*

Association of American University Presses, 71 W. 23rd St., New York, NY 10010. (212) 989-1010. Fax (212) 989-0275. E-mail: aaupny@aol.com. Web page: http://aaupnet.org/ (includes online employment database).

Association of Black Women Historians. E-mail: dickinsg@tcnj.edu. Web page: http://abwh.tcnj.edu/.

Berkshire Conference of Women Historians, Susan Yohn, Secretary/Treasurer, 263 Windsor Pl., Brooklyn, NY 11218. E-mail: smyohn@erols.com. Web page: http://www.berksconference.org.

Committee on Lesbian and Gay History, Marc Stein, Chair, Faculty of Arts, York University, 2140 Vari Hall, 4700 Keele Street, Toronto, ON M3J 1P3, Canada. (416) 736-5123, ext. 66968. E-mail: mrstein@yorku.ca. Web page: http://www.usc.edu/isd/archives/clgh.

Community College Humanities Association, David Berry, Executive Director, c/o Essex County College, 303 University Ave., Newark, NJ 07102. (973) 877-3577. Fax (973) 877-3578. E-mail: dberry6@earthlink.net. Web page: http://www.ccha-assoc.org.

Conference of Historical Journals, Jeannie M. Whayne, Secretary/Treasurer, *Arkansas Historical Quarterly*, Dept. of History, University of Arkansas, Old Main 416, Fayetteville, AR 72701. (501) 575-5884. E-mail: jwhayne@comp.uark.edu. Web page: http://www.h-net.msu.edu/~chj/.

Coordinating Council for Women in History, Rosalind Urbach Moss, Executive Director, PO Box 5401, Saunders Station, Richmond, VA 23220. E-mail: IndeSchol@mindspring.com. Web page: http://www.uoregon.edu /~ccwh.

Editorial Freelancers Association, 71 W. 23rd St., Ste. 1910, New York, NY 10010. (212) 929-5400 / (866) 929-5400. Fax (212) 929-5439 / (866) 929-5439. E-mail: info@the-efa.org. Web page: http://www.the-efa.org.

Educational Testing Service, Rosedale Rd., Princeton, NJ 08541. (609) 921-9000. Fax (609) 734-5410. E-mail: etsinfo@ets.org. Web page: http://www.ets.org.

Federation of State Humanities Councils, 1600 Wilson Blvd., Ste. 902, Arlington, VA 22209. (703) 908-9700. Fax (703) 908-9706. E-mail: humfed@compuserve.com.

H-Net: Humanities and Social Sciences OnLine, Michigan State University, 310 Auditorium, East Lansing, MI 48824-11200. Web page: http://www.h-net.msu.edu (includes online employment database).

Historians Film Committee, Peter C. Rollins, Chair, RR 3, Box 80, Cleveland, OK 74020-9515. (918) 243-7637. Fax (918) 243-5995. E-mail: rollinspc@aol.com. Web page: http://www.h-net.msu.edu/~filmhis/.

Institute of Museum and Library Services, 1100 Pennsylvania Ave., NW, Washington, DC 20506. (202) 606-8536. Fax (202) 606-8591. E-mail: imlsinfo@imls.gov. Web page: http://www.imls.gov.

National Archives and Records Administration, 700 Pennsylvania Ave., NW, Washington, DC 20408-0001. (202) 501-5400 / (866) 325-7208. Web page: http://www.nara.gov.

National Association of Colleges and Employers, 62 Highland Ave., Bethlehem, PA 18017-9085. (610) 868-1421/(800) 544-5272. Fax (610) 868-0208. Web page: http://www.naceweb.org/.

National Coalition of Independent Scholars, Box 5743, Berkeley, CA 94705. Web page: http://www.ncis.org.

National Conference of State Historic Preservation Officers, 444 N. Capitol St., NW, Washington, DC 20001-1512. (202) 624-5465. Fax (202) 624-5419. Web page: http://www.sso.org/ncshpo/.

National Coordinating Committee for the Promotion of History, Bruce Craig, Director, 400 A St., SE, Washington, DC 20003. (202) 544-2422. Fax (202) 544-8307. E-mail: bcraig3@juno.com. Web page: http://www.h-net.msu.edu/~ncc/.

National Council for Preservation Education. Web page: http://www.uvm.edu/histpres/ncpe.

National Council for the Social Studies, 8555 16th Street, Ste. 500, Silver Spring, MD 20910. (301) 588-1800. Web page: http://www.ncss.org.
Publications: *Social Education; Social Studies Professional*

National Council on Public History, Indiana University—Purdue University, 327 Cavanaugh Hall, 425 University Blvd., Indianapolis, IN 46202-5140. (317) 274-2716. E-mail: ncph@iupui.edu. Web page: http://www.ncph.org/.
Publications: *Public History News; The Public Historian*; Barbara J. Howe, *Careers for Students of History; Guide to Graduate Programs in Public History* (1996); *Public History Today* (video)

National Endowment for the Arts, 1100 Pennsylvania Ave., NW, Washington, DC 20506. (202) 682-5400. Web page: http://arts.endow.gov/.

National Endowment for the Humanities, 1100 Pennsylvania Ave., NW, Washington, DC 20506. (202) 606-8400. E-mail: info@neh.gov. Web page: http://www.neh.fed.us.

National Historical Publications and Records Commission, National Archives and Records Administration, 700 Pennsylvania Ave., NW, Rm. 111, Washington, DC 20408-0001. (202) 501-5610. Fax (202) 501-5601. Web page: http://www.nara.gov/nhprc/.

National Register of Historic Places, National Park Service, 1849 C St., NW, NC400, Washington, DC 20240. (202) 343-9536. E-mail: nr_info@nps.gov. Web page: http://www.cr.nps.gov/nr/.

National Society for Experiential Education, 9001 Braddock Road, Ste. 380, Springfield, VA 22151. (703) 426-4268 / (800) 803-4170. Fax (703) 426-8400 / (800) 528-3492. E-mail: info@nsee.org. Web page: http://www.nsee.org.

National Trust for Historic Preservation, 1785 Massachusetts Ave., NW, Washington, DC 20036. (800) 944-6847/(202) 588-6000. Web page: http://www.nthp.org.
Publications: *Preservation;* extensive list of books and pamphlets

Oral History Association, Dickinson College, PO Box 1773, Carlisle, PA 17013. (717) 245-1036. Fax (717) 245-1046. E-mail: oha@dickinson.edu. Web page: http:/omega.dickinson.edu/organizations/oha/.

Organization of American Historians, 112 N. Bryan Ave., Bloomington, IN 47408-4199. (812) 855-7311. Fax (812) 855-0696. E-mail: oah@oah.org. Web page: http://www.oah.org.
Publications: *Journal of American History; OAH Magazine of History; OAH Newsletter; American Stories: Collected Scholarship on Minority History* (1998); *OAH/National Center for History in the Schools Teaching Units*

Organization of History Teachers. Web page: http://users.rcn.com/viceroy1/OHT.htm.

Phi Alpha Theta, Graydon A. Tunstall Jr., Executive Director, University of South Florida, SOC 107, 4202 E. Fowler Ave., Tampa, FL 33620-8100. (610)

336-4925/(800) 394-8195. Fax (610) 336-4929. E-mail: phialpha@ptd.net. Web page: http://www.phialphatheta.org.

Popular Culture Association, Ray B. Browne, Secretary-Treasurer, Bowling Green State University, Bowling Green, OH 43403. (419) 372-2981 / 8095. Web page: http://www.h-net.msu.edu/~pcaaca/popindex.html.

Society for Historians of the Early American Republic, James C. Bradford, Executive Director, Dept. of History, Texas A & M University, College Station, TX 77843-4236. (979) 845-7165. Fax (979) 862-4314. E-mail:jcbradford@tamu.edu.

Society for History Education, PO Box 1578, Borrego Springs, CA 92004. Phone/fax (760) 767-5938. E-mail: cgeorge@julian-ca.com. Web page: http://www.csulb.edu/~histeach/.

Society for History in the Federal Government, Box 14139, Ben Franklin Station, Washington, DC 20044. Web page: http://www.shfg.org.
Publications: *The Federalist; Directory of Federal Historical Programs and Activities* (1998)

Society for Scholarly Publishing, 10200 W. 44th Ave., Ste. 304, Wheat Ridge, CO 80033-2840. (303) 422-3914. Fax (303) 422-8894. E-mail: info@sspnet.org. Web page: http://www.sspnet.org.

Society of American Archivists, 527 S. Wells St., 5th Fl., Chicago, IL 60607-3922. (312) 922-0140. Fax (312) 347-1452. Web page: http://www.archivists.org.
Employment Bulletin Online: http://www.archivists.org/employment
Publications: *American Archivist; Archival Outlook; Planning for the Archival Profession* (1986)

United States Office of Personnel Management, 1900 E St., NW, Washington, DC 20415-0001. (202) 606-1800. Web page: http://www.opm.gov.

Western History Association, University of New Mexico, 1080 Mesa Vista Hall, Albuquerque, NM 87131-1181. (505) 277-5234. Fax (505) 277-6023. E-mail: wha@unm.edu. Web page: http://www.unm.edu/~wha.

Women's National Book Association, 160 Fifth Ave., New York, NY 10010. (212) 675-7805. Fax (212) 989-7542. Web page: http://www.wnba-books.org.